The Science of Self-Discipline

Discover Ways to Finish What You Start and Gain the Willpower, Mental Toughness, and Self-Control to Distinguish Yourself from Others

Table of Contents

Part 1: The Power of Self-Discipline and How to Use This Book 1

Chapter 1: The Biology and Brain Science of Self-Discipline. 5

Chapter 2: Get Real: What Is Pushing Your Buttons? 14

Chapter 3: Navy SEALS Self-Discipline Practices 26

Part 2: Self-Discipline Habits: Master the Fundamentals 32

Chapter 4: How to Diagnose Your Discipline Drains 34

Chapter 5: How to Flex Your "Uncomfortable Muscle" 46

Chapter 6: How to Create a More Disciplined Environment for Yourself 55

Chapter 7: The Relationship You Need to Build with Willpower 62

Chapter 8: Eat Your Vegetables! No, Really. 67

Part 3: Self-Discipline Strategies 77

Chapter 9: Why Your Mindset and Approach Are Everything 79

Chapter 10: Quick Fix Guide: Read in Case of Temptation .88

Chapter 11: Additional Strategies for Success..................... 95

Chapter 12: How to Build Routines and Habits for Ultimate Self-Discipline Summary Guide 103

Part 1: The Power of Self-Discipline and How to Use This Book

What is the difference between the mega-successful and the people struggling to keep up in this world? It can be easy to assume that the people operating at the top of their field have some intrinsic advantages that are beyond the reach of the many, such as inherited wealth and access to resources, fame and a platform to operate on, greater intelligence and better athletic prowess or skill bestowed upon them by genetics, or some other advantage that has given them the leg up in life. While there are plenty who are born with a greater social or physical advantage, they will not be the ones that rise to the top of their field and become great successes and leaders and distinguish themselves in their industry. The people who are able to do this all share the same secret weapon: self-discipline.

In fact, there are many famously notable highly successful individuals who have distinguished themselves in their fields who attribute their high levels of success directly to their self-discipline practices, such as Theodore Roosevelt, Thomas Edison, Vince Lombardi, and Warren Buffet. So, what is self-discipline, exactly?

Self-discipline is defined by the Merriam-Webster dictionary as the power to control one's actions, impulses, and emotions and it is closely associated with many different terms including willpower, self-control, self-restraint, self-government, determination, command, and so many more. At its very core, however, is the truth that self-discipline is controlled entirely by the self. This is wonderful news for you because this means that you and you alone will be the only one with the responsibility of self-discipline, and in this sole responsibility is a great power. It means that *you* are the one in control of this powerful force, and this book will guide you in how to further develop, train, and wield it.

It is an unfortunate reality that so many people consider self-discipline to be a character trait that a person either has or doesn't have, but this could not be further from the truth. Yes, there are some people who are more naturally inclined towards characteristics of self-discipline, but this does not mean that it is not a skill that can be learned, developed, and strengthened through training and practice. Just as some people may be born with natural ease for athletics, others must train their bodies through repetition and guidance to be able to perform at a higher level of success. The same rings true for self-discipline and in fact, self-discipline is what sets apart the pro from the amateur and the expert from the novice. Self-discipline is the key to success in any arena of life, business, or personal.

In this book, you will learn what the biology and brain science behind self-discipline are and how to best support and develop the parts of the brain that are responsible for self-discipline. You will learn how to become honest with yourself in what your triggers are that may stand in the way of you utilizing this incredibly powerful tool in your daily life and you will learn how to overcome them. You will learn about how the elite of the elite military forces in the world- the United States Navy SEALS- structure their lives and careers around this secret weapon and what can be learned about self-discipline by viewing their success strategies, and you will also learn how to better structure your environment to set yourself up for greater success with self-discipline, including diagnosing your "discipline drains," flexing your "uncomfortable muscle" and creating a more disciplined environment, wherever you are. You will learn about the importance of the relationship you have with the important skills of self-discipline such as willpower, self-control, and mental toughness, and how to physically make better choices to support your self-discipline skills. You will better understand how to shift your mindset and your approach to be better equipped to grow your self-discipline muscle in your everyday life, and you will be given tools and techniques to train, develop, practice, and reinforce your self-discipline skills in many different situations and applications.

This book is designed to give you the tools you need to become a master of yourself and by extension, your life and your success. As the ancient philosopher, Plato said, "The first and best victory is to conquer self," and this is the first truth that will become abundantly clear when you build your self-discipline skill set. Once you are master of yourself, you will be unstoppable in your endeavors and will be well on your way to success in completing your goals, whatever they may be. In doing so, you will distinguish yourself from others as being a person that can reach for and attain anything they desire-someone who is virtually unstoppable.

Chapter 1: The Biology and Brain Science of Self-Discipline

To begin to delve into the skill of self-discipline, it must first be understood where it comes from, and this is where biology and brain science come in. The human brain is divided into different areas, or lobes, with each lobe responsible for and associated with specific tasks and functions. The part of the brain associated with decision making, planning, behavior regulation, self-control, and self-discipline is the prefrontal cortex. Interestingly enough, this is the last part of the brain to fully develop in humans, with most neurologists agreeing that this part of the brain does not fully develop until somewhere around the age of 25!

The functions associated with the prefrontal cortex are often termed "executive functions," and these functions are thought to be incredibly important to any sort of planning and conscious effort. It likely goes without saying that self-discipline requires both of these in generous amounts. A person must first make the plan for whatever it is that they are pursuing, and then must apply the effort to that practice consciously. These executive functions of the prefrontal cortex are considered to be fully developed around the age of 25, but even in the years before and after this, this area of the brain can still be changed, and these functions can be further developed and strengthened.

To better understand this process we must understand neuroplasticity or the reality that the brain is not a fixed organ; the structure of the brain can be changed as neurons, or brain cells, are wired together in different ways depending on the neural pathways that they take as they communicate with one another. This process is called neurotransmission. To further explain this, neural pathways can be likened to a hiking trail in the forest. Most people will choose to stay on the so-called beaten path, the one where the brambly bushes have been cut back, and the pine cones have been kicked to the side. To cut through the thick of the forest would be a more difficult path, so most people will choose to stay on the well-cleared hiking trail. Who wants to take the path that involves the low hanging branches that we have to duck under to avoid being slapped in the face and the large root systems underfoot that slow us down as we carefully step over them? Just as we make this choice while hiking, our neurons, or brain cells, do the same as they communicate to one another throughout our lives.

Every action or reaction a person makes is one neuron communicating to another neuron which communicates to another neuron and so on and so on and so on. These communication paths, or neural pathways, are often so well-worn and used so frequently that we don't think twice about the action we are taking. As a (hopefully, at least!) universal example, we can take a look at daily hygiene habits. Most people brush their teeth twice a day and shower or bathe several times a week. During these hygiene rituals, most people operate on what can be referred to as an "autopilot" mode that doesn't require a lot of conscious thought. Think back to the last time you brushed your teeth. Do you recall having an inner dialogue in which you thought about how you were picking up your toothbrush, picking up the tube of toothpaste, removing the cap, squeezing the toothpaste out, replacing the cap, bringing the toothbrush up to your mouth, inserting the toothbrush into your mouth, and beginning to brush? Probably not, right? Most of us might instead find our minds wandering as we think of essentially anything but the actual steps of what we are doing! This is because a tooth brushing is a consistent action that is performed twice a day, every day, for the entirety of a person's life. This is something that is done so frequently and with a certain amount of predictability and expectation that people don't need to consciously think about it while they do it.

The neural pathways involved in tooth brushing are well-worn and regularly traveled, and these habitual daily tasks that are automated for us by our brain processes save us enormous amounts of time and effort by happening without much of our conscious effort and planning. Combine this with the connections to the physical movements of our arms, hands, and mouth, also sometimes referred to as muscle memory, and this helps to facilitate mental autopilot.

However, let's imagine now that your dentist has just told you that rather than floss first, brush teeth second, and use mouthwash last, they would like you to instead begin with mouthwash first, floss second, then brush teeth last. This restructuring of your routine would probably require a certain amount of concerted effort on your part. The first few times you would go to brush your teeth you would likely feel a little awkward interrupting your unconscious actions and you would need to be thinking of the sequence of events that you were going to do because you would need to go against the well-traveled neural pathway that you have programmed into yourself over the years. For most, this process of retraining the brain and forging new neural pathways will take many repetitions. Once the new neural pathway has been formed and strengthened, the action can be considered habitual or automatic. In this way, many of our daily tasks are completed with little to no conscious efforts on our part.

Try this experiment the next time you go to hop in the shower or bath. Change the sequence in which you normally clean yourself. Maybe instead of washing your hair first and then washing your body second, instead swap them, so you wash your body first and your hair second. Commit to doing this for three weeks by marking it on your calendar or penciling it into your planner. Track and take note of how long it takes for this new routine or sequence to feel natural and less forced. Psychologists, researchers, and time management specialists suggest that it typically takes about twenty-one days for a new habit to be established. At what point during your experiment do you start to feel as if this new behavior may be becoming a habit? What do you suppose will happen after the three-week period if you decide to go back to your original bath and shower routine? Do you think you might seamlessly fall back into your old habits or will it take just as long to go back to the old routine as it did to build the habit of the new routine? Most people find that it can be easier to go back to the old routine than it was to build the new routine, as the old neural pathways that were formed had been built and used over a period of many, many years and numerous repetitions, whereas the new neural pathways have only been used about twenty-one times or so.

The key here to forming the new neural pathways is repetition and consistency. There will always be a period of time where the new actions- in this case, the new acts of self-discipline- will feel somewhat forced and perhaps even unauthentic. This is normal, natural, and necessary and will likely happen every time you push yourself beyond your comfort level. It is important to remain committed and consistent in the pursuit of the new action in order to strengthen the neural pathways for the neurotransmission to occur on, and eventually, there will come a time when this behavior no longer requires the same sort of conscious force and effort. Eventually, you will be able to draw on your new skills in autopilot mode, similarly to how you brush your teeth or take a shower. The key to learning anything is always repetition and consistency!

In addition to building and reinforcing the neural networks and pathways, there are other practices that can be done to build the brain into a stronger, more efficient machine that is more capable of practicing self-discipline. One of the very simplest is to meditate.

Meditation has some very concrete benefits for the brain. In fact, researchers from the University of Wisconsin found that meditation increases gray matter in the brain, particularly in the region of the prefrontal cortex, which is the part of the brain responsible for those executive functions such as planning and conscious effort; this is the part that will be crucial for developing and strengthening the necessary aspects of self-discipline: self-control, decision making, willpower, and behavior regulation.

It is well known among healthcare professionals that humans lose gray matter as they age, and various areas of the brain will shrink. This is part of the reason why it is natural for humans to get more forgetful as they age, but this is not the case for people who meditate regularly. In fact, when reviewing brain scans of fifty-year-old meditators to twenty-five-year-old meditators, it can be seen that they still have the same amount of gray matter, particularly in the prefrontal cortex!

Some people may assume that the fifty-year-old meditators were "professional" meditators that were highly trained in this practice. However, there was an additional study done to test this very aspect that compared two groups of people, one who had been assigned an eight-week program in mindfulness training and practice which included daily meditation and the other which was not. At the end of the eight weeks, the researchers found differences in the amount of gray matter and thickening of different regions in the region, as the brain built new connections and neural pathways for the mindfulness meditation group. Regular meditation practices have the same benefits for a novice as they do for a professional, and via neuroimaging, these brain-boosting differences can be seen as clear as day!

Meditation not only increases and supports executive functions of the brain, but also leads to a decrease in stress overall, an increased level of happiness, increased reports of success and pride in personal pursuits, deeper and more fulfilling sleep, better problem-solving skills, and decreased anxiety. The many benefits of meditation all contribute to a brain that is functioning at peak utility and is better able to handle daily stressors and avoid the potential pitfalls and obstacles that can often occur to challenge a person's self-discipline.

In fact, there is a correlation between building better self-discipline skills and decreased stress and anxiety. This is due to the reality that living an undisciplined life in which a person does not feel as if they are in the pilot's seat of their own life often contributes to stress and anxiety! The key takeaway here is that there is a mutually beneficial relationship between self-discipline skills and stress and anxiety levels. If a person does not have much self-discipline, their stress and anxiety levels will likely be higher than a person with stronger self-discipline skills. If a person has high stress and anxiety levels, it will likely be harder for them to practice their self-discipline skills. However, if a person works hard to build their self-discipline skills, their stress and anxiety levels will decrease! If a person works to bring down their stress and anxiety levels, their ability to better utilize their self-discipline skills will also increase.

This relationship between self-discipline and stress and anxiety is an important relationship for people to be aware of as they embark on their journey to build better self-discipline skills. It is important that a person pursuing better self-discipline skills is aware of these connections so their practical pursuit can be maximized.

Now you have learned how neuroplasticity allows our brains to grow and strengthen skills depending on our practices. Anytime you are building new skills, including skills such as self-discipline, it is important that we perform the skills we are building repeatedly so these neural pathways in our brains can be strengthened with repetition and consistency. In addition to strengthening the neural pathways our neurons take during neurotransmission; it is also important to strengthen our brains with practices like meditation and mindfulness.

Meditation not only increases the gray matter of the brain in areas such as the prefrontal cortex that executive function such as planning and conscious effort are associated with, but it also decreases the stress and anxiety in life that will hinder and inhibit self-discipline practices. Meditation is associated with better focus and control and this is a part of the reason why so many successful business people and entrepreneurs cite it as being an integral part of their success, such as Oprah Winfrey, daytime TV talk show host who created her own brand that includes a television network, a magazine, a school, and so much more, and billionaire Jeff Bezos of the Amazon empire. Meditation should be considered as a part of an essential daily brain work-out that primes us to complete our tasks efficiently and successfully, and self-discipline skills are included in this. In order to finish what you start and gain the willpower, mental toughness, and self-control to distinguish yourself from others, you must do all you can to build and strengthen your brain!

Chapter 2: Get Real: What Is Pushing Your Buttons?

Most everyone is familiar with the phrase "having your buttons pushed." It is a common colloquial phrase referring to the experience of being exposed to irritants that trigger unsavory reactions in ourselves, such as anger and annoyance. It takes a certain level of maturity and self-discipline in order to effectively avoid allowing yourself to react to this sort of experience, and this is an important step in building the crucial self-discipline skills of willpower, mental toughness, and self-control.

Have you heard the phrase, "know thyself" before? It is crucial to know yourself and what your weak points are in order to leave effective coping strategies to handle them. To begin this chapter, think back to times in your life when you have reacted to an irritant in an angry or annoying way that was beyond your conscious control. If you are able, make a list of five distinct such reactions. Follow the template below and be sure to save it and set it aside for use later.

BUTTONS PUSHED	ANSWER
Where was I?	Be specific in
How old was I?	Your answers
Who was involved?	Here! It is
What happened?	Important to

How did I react?	Include as
How did other people react?	Much detail
How did it feel afterward?	As you can
How can I change my reaction?	Remember!

The chart above provides the template for you to dig in and look at the ways you have had your buttons pushed in the past and the ways in which you reacted that you might not have been particularly proud of that you would want to change if you could. Developing self-discipline only happens when a person is prepared and aware of their own personal tendencies.

Be as thorough as you can in your responses. Set aside a chunk of time in which you can accurately complete this chart as honestly and completely as you are able to. In the "Where was I?" section, be sure to include details about your setting, including what time of day it was. In the "How old was I?" section, be sure to be as accurate as you can be. When answering "Who was involved," be sure to include people who may not have been directly involved in the button-pushing but also may have simply been there and witnessed the incident. You will see why this is important later! When you answer "What happened," be sure to include the lead-up, such as notable events that may have occurred earlier that day. If it was a comment someone made that set you off, be sure to include what was being talked about beforehand or what everyone was doing when the comment was made. In the "How did I react?"

section, including both what you said, did, and felt at the time of the incident. In the "How did other people react?" section, including what other people said, did, and looked like at the time, to the best of your recollection. In the "How did I feel afterward?" section, include both how it felt immediately afterward and how it feels now as you look back at it. Leave the "How can I change my reaction" space blank for now!

The purpose of looking back at the ways in which our buttons have been pushed before is so we can study those experiences for important information you will need to now be able to cultivate the self-discipline skills you are working on. It is a normal human reaction to experience annoyance and even sometimes anger at life's irritants, whether it is something another person said or did or a natural event that occurs such as rain canceling a long-awaited for the day at the beach or an elevator being broken that forces you to take the stairs. What is not normal is allowing those triggers to inspire a reaction out of us that is beyond our control. This is not embodying the mental toughness, willpower, and self-control that are both so crucial to self-discipline.

Now that you have completed your chart, set it off to the side. You will refer back to this later to check progress. For now, it is enough that you have thought back in detail to the times in your life when you lacked the self-discipline to avoid reacting to these types of triggers.

What is it about certain scenarios, situations, and people that can inspire these big feelings that are then acted upon with little to no conscious action? Everyone carries a long memory of personal history that includes negative experiences from the past, and when we don't take effort to consciously heal from and untangle the big feelings we had surrounding that negative experience, then we can find ourselves overreacting to people or events pushing our buttons later in situations that are entirely unrelated to the original event in question.

The way to address this is to first be honest with ourselves and where these big feelings have come from. Look at the first item on your list. Note the circumstances of what happened; the where, the who, the why, and the how. Now think of other times in your life, prior to that situation, that you have experienced similar scenarios. Often, these other situations have happened when we were very young and extra sensitive to situations that cause stress and likely did not have as many tools for dealing with stress in a constructive or healthy manner.

Sometimes these situations may not seem directly related on a superficial level and may require extra work and consideration on your part to figure out where they originated from. For example, if your "pushing your buttons" scenario is about a co-worker that made an off-hand comment about clocking in late for a shift, then you will need to look beyond that particular scenario. Perhaps it requires looking more in-depth at the relationship that you have with that particular co-worker; does that co-worker have a contentious history with you in which they often make comments that you consider to be overly critical and disrespectful? Or does the problem in question perhaps come from a scenario entirely unrelated to work? Perhaps you need to look back to other scenarios in your life in which you have had people make comments about mistakes that upset you; maybe your mother made comments about incidents that were not overly critical or a big deal in the sense that you would remember one large and difficult experience, but the accumulation of all of the small and off-hand critical comments created a response in you which is hypersensitive to what you perceive as unnecessary off-hand critical comments. This would be a scenario in which the undisciplined response you had to the co-worker is likely a direct result of being unconscious of this response in yourself.

By examining the circumstances surrounding each instance in which you have found your self-discipline lacking when it comes to these big reactions from having your buttons pushed, you will be able to work towards a mindful response instead of a mindless reaction. The difference here will be in the understanding of why it is that that particular scenario is causing annoyance and frustration and in the conscious effort that will be required to design and enact a different response.

Sadly, many of us walk through life without taking the time or effort to look more closely at the reasons why we have the reactions we do. Some people believe that in order to be mentally tough, they must deny that they are carrying emotional baggage that continues to affect them. It should go without saying that self-discipline is required to have a measured and careful response, but even amongst people who consider themselves to be fairly self-disciplined, there can still be a lack of awareness into how their history has affected them and how their triggers are still calling the shots in certain situations.

To avoid this same fate, it will be important to begin to practice a few new techniques when it comes to communication with others and how you relate to the world around you. In daily communication, it can be helpful to set a new personal intention. As you communicate with others, make it a part of your new practice to hear their words- and only their words- rather than trying to read the meaning beyond the words. For example, if a person calls out to you, "nice shirt!" accept that they were giving you a compliment on your shirt. Do not allow yourself to try and read more into the words they said and imagine that they might be mocking you by being sarcastic, even if you've had that experience before at some point in your life and now feel particularly sensitive about that. In order to maintain clear communication with other people, we must begin to separate out our own baggage from the relationship at hand in order to see it and experience it as it truly is rather than how we fear or imagine it to be.

Focus on direct communication and commit yourself to not only hearing the direct message being given to you but also to saying directly what you mean rather than veiling meaning under sarcasm and innuendo. In doing so, you will be restructuring your brain to expect more honesty and clarity in communication and releasing old patterns and habits of suspecting and dissecting hidden meaning. Remember that each new person you interact with is a new relationship and doesn't carry any of the same baggage of your old relationships, whatever they might have been.

Another useful tool in priming yourself to avoid having your buttons pushed is to try to structure and steer conversations and experiences in directions that you know will not trigger you. If you find that political conversations tend to make you very reactive, then excuse yourself when the conversation turns to politics or just drop a friendly disclaimer that you do not like to discuss politics because it has a tendency to upset you and you'd like to talk about something else instead. If the people around you respect that and shift gears, great! If not, excuse yourself from the conversation politely.

If you know that you have sensitivity during crowded parties and have a tendency to feel particularly defensive in spaces where you are physically restricted, then you can easily avoid these types of situations or set up your appearances at parties and places such as this in a mindful way. For example, you might decide that you will hang out by a door or an open window in an attempt to manage the feeling the sort of physical restriction that can put you in a position where you will easily feel your buttons being pushed. Remember that it is ultimately your responsibility to take care of yourself and avoid being triggered; it is never another person's responsibility to take care of you in this way.

It is also a part of your responsibility to understand that communication can get very complicated! There are many different ways that people communicate with one another, and an ideal way to cultivate communication styles that contribute to self-discipline is to stay present at the moment and focus on what is being said in that very moment. Resist the temptation to think back to previous conversations that you have already had with this person or similar conversations you have had with others or to project forward into what you think this conversation may mean. By focusing on remaining present and in the moment, you can flex your self-discipline muscle in the event that something is said or done that pushes your buttons.

There are times when these minor irritants and annoyances of life that push our buttons may be sending us an important message, and it is important to take a moment and try to determine if there is something there that we need to learn. For example, sometimes the things that are pushing our buttons are doing so because we need to do better at setting limits for ourselves. Perhaps you have encountered someone that seems to not recognize your boundaries by asking questions that are far too personal to you, and you feel annoyed at being asked about it. Rather than allow yourself to react in a non-disciplined way, instead focus on asserting your boundaries in a polite but firm way, perhaps by saying something like, "I'd really rather not talk about that with you." This asserts your boundaries and needs and sets up the relationship and yourself for future success.

There may also be times where something is pushing our buttons that is reminding us that we need to protect our time and space. This could be an overzealous neighbor that likes to rush out of their door when they see you pull in to have a conversation with you, even if you are obviously returning home from a long day at work and are carrying grocery bags. This situation could potentially end in fireworks in which you eventually overreact angrily about the other person's inability to respect your time and space, or you can act to assert yourself before the situation gets that far. You could strategize in the car on the way home about what you will say if your neighbor comes out again, again asserting your boundaries in a polite, but firm way. It is important to remember that asserting your boundaries before you have your buttons pushed is the ideal way to keep your responses measured and disciplined. Once your buttons have been pushed, it can be much harder to cultivate a disciplined response.

Sometimes the things that push our buttons serve as timely reminders that the way we are doing something needs to be restructured. Maybe a daily irritant of a crowded subway platform can be easily avoided by restructuring your morning routine to leave the house ten minutes earlier, which would take the pressure off of making it through the crowds. Or maybe the daily irritant of finding parking could be avoided by carpooling with a neighbor or catching rideshare to work. Often times, these life annoyances can serve as important reminders that something needs a change.

It can be helpful to take a meaningful look at the things that are pushing your buttons regularly and consider where you might be able to shift things around to take the pressure off. Could it be that maybe the dirty clothes scattered on your child's floor are only a symptom of a greater problem? It's not the dirty clothes on the floor that is the ultimate problem here, but rather the issue beyond the dirty clothes on the floor. Is it that you are feeling as if you are not receiving any help around the house? Is it that you are worried your child is not learning responsibility and how to pull their fair share around the house? Try to get to the root of the issue at hand and address that. Sit down and have meaningful and actionable conversations about how to tweak problem situations to prevent the trigger from occurring over and over again.

On occasion, a person who is regularly triggered into undisciplined reactions might also be suffering from perfectionism. It is well worth it to take a step back and reexamine priorities in your life to ensure that the issue is not that you are heaping too high of an expectation in different areas or trying to force people into roles they are not ready to play. For example, could it be that your standard of cleanliness is higher than average and in order to maintain that while working full-time outside of the home will require outsourcing some of that work or shifting your expectation? Could it be that your expectation of your children's behavior is beyond what they are developmentally capable of and perhaps you might need to relax your expectations some to accommodate what is age-appropriate behavior? Either way, perfectionism is a trait that goes hand in hand with undisciplined responses because attempting to get everything perfectly right all of the time is a disastrous recipe for eventual blow-ups.

Now that you have read the many ways you can shift your reaction; go back to the chart you filled out at the beginning of this chapter and go through and fill out how you can change the responses should you encounter those scenarios again. It is important to be specific and make actionable steps you can take so that way the next time you find yourself in a similar spot, it will be easy to make the choice of what you should do. Think back to how your expectations or your actions might need to shift in order to set yourself up for ultimate success, and then practice how you might change them in the future both by engaging in visualization and dress-rehearsal style strategies. The more pre-homework you can complete before you are put in the position of confronting these triggers that push your buttons, the better off you will be to act with the self-discipline that is necessary to finish what you start and get what you want by using the willpower, mental toughness, and self-control to distinguish yourself from others.

Chapter 3: Navy SEALS Self-Discipline Practices

Navy SEALS, the United States Navy Sea, Air, and Land teams are the U.S. Navy's elite special operations force and a part of the Naval Special Warfare Command. Navy SEALS are the teams that are called in to perform both the guerrilla and non-guerrilla style warfare, the highly specialized and high stakes military options in the military. One of the most well-known aspects of Navy SEALS are the incredibly strict, structured, and disciplined training standards they have even compared to the rest of the U.S. military's high standards. If there is one thing that Navy SEALS are known for around the world, it is their self-discipline.

Navy SEAL training is extraordinarily rigorous and demanding. Their attrition rate, or the rate of the number of people who fail out of the program and must be recycled to start all over again or be placed into another program, lies at about 80%. That means about 80% of the people who go through the Navy SEAL program will not make it all the way out without failure! It typically takes about a year for a soldier to make their way through this incredibly taxing and harsh U.S. Navy SEAL training program.

Their training program begins with a twenty-four-week school known as Basic Underwater Demolition/SEAL (BUD/S) school, in which trainees are required to put their mental and physical stamina and leadership skills to the ultimate test. There are three distinct phases intended to become more demanding as the trainee passes through each one. They cover physical conditioning exercises, combat diving exercises, and land warfare exercises.

A significant part of the Navy SEALS BUD/S training is designed to essentially put the candidates in situations that are so incredibly intense that they would break most people physically and mentally. The people that do persevere and succeed under this level of intensity- that elite 20%- are then considered to be tough and resilient enough to perform the kinds of tasks that active-duty Navy SEALS will be given throughout their service. It is the ultimate in make it or break it techniques, and because of this, Navy SEALS are considered to be the absolute toughest of the tough in the United States military.

It is said that most people have a common misconception about this high-intensity training, particularly the first week that is often referred to as "Hell Week," and that is that it is mostly testing the physical strength and endurance of the candidates. BUD/S instructors say this could not be further from the truth. The ultimate thing that is being tested for is mental strength and endurance.

The physical situations that the trainees are put in are designed to push mental toughness and self-discipline to the absolute max. Candidates are put through extreme physical conditioning such as having their hands and feet tied together and being put into water so they can learn how to become "drown-proof." Candidates are forced to endure frigid temperatures by breaking through solid ice, treading water for 3-4 minutes, then getting themselves out of the icy water and completing an additional survival task. Candidates endure an entire week of sleep deprivation and extreme physical and mental limit testing, and it is all done to ensure that each trainee that makes it through is able to withstand the extreme situations that Navy SEALS find themselves in during the course of their duty.

According to David Goggins, esteemed former Navy SEAL turned motivational speaker and writer:

"It's so easy to be great nowadays because everyone else is weak. If you have ANY mental toughness, if you have any fraction of self-discipline; the ability to not want to do it, but still do it; if you can get through to doing things that you hate to do: on the other side is GREATNESS."

This is a person that survived Hell Week- not once, not twice, but THREE times before he completed it- and pushed himself to the absolute limits of human endurance both during his time with the Navy SEALS and also outside of the Navy SEALS. Goggins' personal story is an inspirational testament to the power of mental toughness and self-discipline. He talks of how he grew up in immense poverty and physical abuse, struggled with health challenges such as sickle cell anemia and a congenital heart defect and one day saw a commercial on television for the Navy SEAL program and told himself that he would do that someday, despite the fact that at the time he weighed over 300 pounds and was incredibly out of shape both mentally and physically. However, he made up his mind that very day that that was what he was going to do with his life, and he was ruthless in his pursuit of mental and physical improvement and success.

David Goggins has built an empire that consists of sharing his personal mental toughness and self-discipline strategies and wisdom, and he has stated that training the mind is far more important than training the body. Goggins states that just as a body becomes callused physically, so too does the mind when it is used properly. Looking back at the Navy SEALS training program, this is what the program is essentially designed to do: to callus the mind. The people who will complete the training and become Navy SEALS must be able to be counted on to perform the missions that they are tasked with; there cannot be a risk of people falling apart mentally or physically in the middle of an important mission, so the training program is designed to push them to their limits and force them to both extend and overextend their abilities, so they can experience being pushed and stretched in this way to see if they are up to the task. Without the mental toughness and self-discipline to push through the enormity of the physical expectations, most people fall apart when pushed to these extremes.

Another notable former Navy SEAL turned motivational speaker and writer, Jocko Willink, has also created a brand that espouses the lessons that he learned as a Navy SEAL as his secret to success, and he touts discipline as being the only universal ingredient that anyone needs to meet their goals. Willink believes that discipline will always beat motivation because motivation is fleeting, while a well-built skill set of discipline lasts forever and can be applied to everything in a person's life.

These are people who have made it through the most excruciating fitness and psychological training programs on the planet and came out of the other side to tell the world that the one skill set that they needed to be successful in their endeavors- both in the Navy SEALS and beyond- was discipline. Not just discipline, but self-discipline. It does no one any good if they are only able to stay on task and complete their goals because another person is standing over them and forcing them to stay on track. The commitment to oneself and the ability to push through whatever temporary pain and sacrifice stands between a person and their goals is necessary to build the strong, life-long self-discipline that former Navy SEALS such as David Goggins and Jocko Willink know is the key to living a life where the barriers between a person and what they want out of life no longer matter; there is no barrier that is insurmountable when a person has the self-discipline to push themselves to the task.

Navy SEALS are not Navy SEALS because they are strong and physically fit. They are not Navy SEALS because they had instructors standing over them, forcing them to complete their tasks. They are Navy SEALS because they cultivated and built the self-discipline that is required to push themselves through whatever task was handed to them, no matter how large or how daunting. Navy SEALS don't give up because a task is difficult; Navy SEALS call on the self-discipline and mental toughness that keeps them relentlessly driving forward no matter the physical and mental challenge. Everyone is capable of taking themselves to the next level of their career, of their relationships, of their fitness journeys, of their lives, by learning and living these same strategies and game plans that Navy SEALS do.

Part 2: Self-Discipline Habits: Master the Fundamentals

Self-discipline is powerful. It requires mental toughness, willpower, self-control, and internal motivation. In order to gain control and mastery over this incredibly powerful weapon, a person must learn the fundamentals of self-discipline and the tools necessary to put them into practice.

Many people hear or read about self-discipline and assume that it can be a skill that a person practices a few times to complete a project or two, and then they can put it back on the shelf, and it will be there for their use the next time they might need it. It is true that they might be able to have some level of self-discipline that works that way, but if you are looking to take your life to the next level, self-discipline fundamentals must be learned and mastered in a way that makes them habitual. Not a superficially habitual skill, either, but a deeply ingrained and inspired way to live and act in all areas of your life: personal goals, business goals, relationships, everything.

There are many different tactics and strategies for building self-discipline skills, but they will not do a thing until a person has successfully mastered the fundamentals of self-discipline habits, and this is what part two will cover. You will learn how to diagnose and understand the parts of your life that are zapping your discipline willpower and how to adjust these aspects for better success. You will read about why it is a fundamentally important part of self-discipline to be able to sit in the discomfort of a moment and how to both flex and strengthen this muscle in your life. You will learn how to better create and cultivate a disciplined environment to set yourself up for the best chance at success in whatever you are pursuing. You will also learn about how the relationships in our life can all be used and utilized to build your self-discipline. Even a negative relationship has its place! Lastly, you will learn about how even what you put in your body will affect your discipline levels in a major way and how to take care of yourself in the best possible way for maximum success.

By learning to master the fundamentals in your self-discipline habits, you will understand how to gain the willpower, mental toughness, and self-control to finish what you start and distinguish yourself from others.

Chapter 4: How to Diagnose Your Discipline Drains

What is a discipline drain? Well, what is a drain on anything? A drain is anything that uses up or siphons away a resource. Take a moment to visualize the drain in your bathtub at home. It doesn't matter how much water you continue to pour in via the faucet, if the drain is open, you will never be able to fill the tub with enough water to take a bath.

The discipline drains in your life are the very same. It does not matter how much willpower, self-control, motivation, and mental strength you pour into a task, if there is a discipline drain sucking away these valuable resources, you will never be able to hit the goals you are reaching in a meaningful and impactful way. It is a waste of your resources.

In order to prevent this from kneecapping you and blocking the progress you know you can make in life, you must first take a long and honest look around you to see what your discipline drains may be.

So what are the parts of your life that are holding you back and keeping you from utilizing the mental toughness, willpower, and self-control that you need to better develop and strengthen in order to finish what you start and distinguish yourself from others? Where are you wasting your resources?

A common drain that almost every person on the planet must overcome is fear. Fear does not have to be an externally ominous and aggressive thing, like fear of oncoming category 5 hurricanes that we are in the path of. Fear can also be the fear that sneaks into the corner of your mind that you aren't even entirely aware is there, and this is where self-awareness again becomes very important. Fear can be the voice in the back of your head that points out that you are starting later than other successful people in your industry or the feeling you get when you hear someone else mentioning the resources necessary for the venture you are embarking on and you know you won't have easy access to them.

There are some that feel that fear is a motivating force that can be useful, and this is true to a certain point. However, fear is a negative motivating factor and while it can prove useful to inspire a person to get an initial boost in energy, it will eventually zap that energy and will work against a person and their self-discipline.

It is important that people recognize this and work to put their fears in proper perspective. Like so many other negative emotions, fear only has the power than you give it. Once you take the wind out of its sails, so to speak, it will no longer have the same energy-zapping power over you that it once had. In order to defuse the power that your fears might hold over you, take a moment to engage in the fear power-busting exercise below that is designed to release you from the power that these potential fears may hold over you.

YOUR FEAR	THE VERY WORST THING THAT COULD HAPPEN
Use this space to	Over here write out the very worst thing that could happen if your fear
List the fears	Comes true. Be as detailed as you can. If your fear is that you might lose
You currently	Your job, describe the repercussions of that. Will you lose your home, your
Have in all	Car, your gym membership, etc.? Will relationships become more stressful if
Areas of your	Does this happen? Will you find your future retirement compromised in specific
Life:	Ways? Be as clear and specific as you can so you can
Professional,	completely visualize and
Personal, and	See the ways in which your fears could potentially play out.
elsewhere	

For some people, this exercise can be difficult to complete, but it is such a fruitful exercise! The importance of this exercise is in diffusing the power of your fears. Once you have described, in detail, the ways that your life could be impacted in the event that your very worst fears come true, then you have taken some of the ominous concern out of that fear. You have already seen what will happen if your worst fear would come true and you can see that despite whatever fear was present, you are still standing and can continue to fight your battle the next day. Do not let fear take up more of the precious metal resources that you have.

Another common discipline drain that many people share is envy. Envy, however, has two sides. One side of envy is a malicious, resentful feeling where we feel some anger towards the person for what they have or what they have accomplished, and it makes us wish them ill or think less of them because they have something we do not. The other side of envy can be quite benign, where a person sees what another person has and recognizes that it is something that they also want to either have or accomplish, and this benign envy can be a very motivating factor as it can inspire us to move towards our goals, too.

If the envy you feel is malicious and you are experiencing jealousy and resentment towards another person, these are the emotions that will drain your resources. This must be moved on from, and you will need to flip the script on your envy from one of resentment of another and their accomplishments to one where you use them as a case study for the possibilities in life that you can also achieve! You can even choose to take the envy you feel and ask the object of envy to share their story with you and maybe even take on a mentorship role with you. You can also study their life from afar if you don't have the kind of relationship where requesting mentorship would be possible. Pay attention to the resources they used and look into how these could be valuable for you as well.

Another discipline drain that occurs for people is an electronic distraction. Even if your industry requires you to frequently check your email and social media, you must be willing to disconnect from these electronic distractions regularly. Otherwise, the never-ending newness of scrolling through a Twitter or Facebook feed that never ends will keep your brain primed for that constant dopamine hit of "What's this?" and "Look at that!" without allowing yourself to relax and recalibrate your thoughts. It is being studied more and more how the never-ending attachment to electronics and scrolling through lists of "ten best this" or "the newest that" is affecting the pleasure centers of our brains and how we can become quite dependent on these dopamine hits to keep ourselves coming back for more and more. The problem here is that scrolling through Instagram, and other social media sites is essentially a time drain. It also contributes to discipline draining emotions such as envy and fear. Smart utilization of resources is key to building the skillsets necessary for active self-discipline.

A discipline drain that can be easily avoided for most is overwhelming. When a person is embarking on a major endeavor, whether it is a lofty fitness goal or the start of a challenging career path like the opening of a business, it can be easy to get ahead of oneself. For example, many people like to stretch out the list of things that they need to do before them and put everything together as a task that needs to happen before their goal is met. This can, unfortunately, create an unnecessary amount of pressure on a person.

Rather than allow all of the tasks that must be completed to exist as a non-structured grouping of tasks that must be completed before goals are met, instead break down the tasks into individual goals. If the goal is to file incorporation papers for your new business, but you must first meet with your lawyer, meet with your business partner, make three different phone calls, and e-sign some documents, separate each of these things out into their own individual goal. List the items that must be completed in the order they should be completed as their own individual goal, and as you go through the list, mark each item off.

There are two reasons this is so effective at avoiding overwhelm. One is that it follows the old adage of the best way to eat an elephant: one bite at a time! Any large task that seems insurmountable can only be accomplished one step at a time. The second reason this is effective is that it allows for momentum to form and build on itself. The most difficult step is always the first step, but once a person gets moving towards a goal, it gets easier to keep moving. Let your momentum build from a snowball to an avalanche and see how much easier it is to maintain willpower and self-control to complete the tasks you start!

A discipline drain that can happen to people that start off strong and motivated in their goal pursuit is one of limited perspective. Occasionally you may find that you get very excited to begin a new pursuit and you may find that it is very easy to take actions towards completing this goal as it often seems in the beginning as if the energy and motivation to be productive is limitless. The roadblocks and obstacles that may lie ahead may seem unimportant or trivial as you look ahead with the rose-colored glasses that many people wear at the beginning of a project. However, as the project moves forward and hiccups happen, it may seem as if reality comes crashing down and momentum slows. Once momentum slows, it can feel like something is not working out correctly. It might feel as if something must be fundamentally wrong with the pursuit since it is no longer as easy as it was to continue on the path, but this is where it is necessary to evaluate perspective and shift if necessary.

All too often, people view their goals and their dreams as if they are running a sprint, one in which they must dash as quickly as they can to the finish line. In truth, this is rarely the way anyone finds their way to success. While it may seem less glamorous and attractive, the truth is that the path to success is more often like a marathon than a sprint. It requires a lot of energy and effort, but at a sustainable pace. If a person tries to sprint right out of the gate and expends all of their energy and wears themselves out, it is likely that they will need to stop all efforts to regroup again. Rather than end up in that position, be methodical in the approach of your goals and take care to keep a level of effort up that can be maintained in the long game. There is no prize given out for quickest ascent, the only prize is the one we earn for ourselves in feelings of pride and accomplishment, and any job worth doing is worth right.

Worry is a sure-fire discipline drain. The only thing that worry will do is fill your brain and body with stress chemicals like cortisol that contribute to brain fog and physical fatigue. It is counterproductive to spend your energy actively daydreaming about the things that could potentially go wrong. If you are particularly prone to worry, then be sure to complete the exercise from the beginning of the chapter in which you write out each of your fears to take the heat out of them. You cannot allow your fears to grow larger than they should be, because worry will drain the energy out of you mentally and physically.

Hand in hand with worrying are other negative emotional responses such as doubt, sadness, despair, shame, guilt, and frustration. The problem with these emotional responses is that not only do they all contribute to the stress response mentioned above that can suck the energy out of a person, but they also don't do much to improve a person's willpower, mental toughness, or self-control.

In fact, according to the American Academy of Family Physicians, negative emotional states and responses have very real connections to physical symptoms such as back pain, chest pain, digestive issues and upsets, fatigue, general aches and pains, headaches, high blood pressure, insomnia, sexual issues, breathing issues, weight gain or weight loss. It goes without saying that these physical symptoms would not contribute in a positive way to a person's pursuit of self-discipline if they are otherwise distracted with getting their physical health back on track.

Related to negative emotional states that act as potential discipline drains, there is an activity that often leads to negative emotional states that can act as a potential discipline drain: Gossiping and starting "drama." The act of gossiping and or/engaging in talking badly about others, discussing people's personal lives, telling secrets that have the likelihood of injuring another, these are all things that can serve as potential discipline drains. Aside from often leading to negative emotional states, it immediately takes your focus off of yourself and your goals. Any extraneous attention that is being placed on other people and their lives in an idle manner is not serving any purpose for yourself (or others) that will build and cultivate the mental toughness, self-control, and willpower that you will need to develop a strong self-discipline skill set.

There are many other mental factors that can influence a person's self-discipline and willpower, including taking things personally, holding on to the past, being too near-sighted, being too controlling in other aspects of your life, going through difficult experiences in other areas of your life such as grief over loss of a loved one or concern over a catastrophic financial setback.

This discipline drains may seem and are fairly innocuous one at a time. It is very rare, however, that they occur only one at a time! The greater reality is that in any typical day, most of us encounter any number of these discipline drains. That is why it then becomes important for us to remember how to shift our perspective and guard against this various discipline drains. If you are carrying big fears all day, every day, use the chart to help release and dissipate some of the power behind the fears. If you find yourself feeling envious of someone, spend it a little time being more thoughtful about why you are envious and what exactly the feelings you are experiencing are. Is it a malevolent feeling of resentment and jealousy or a benign feeling of awe and wonder that the person was able to complete a goal that is similar to the goals you are also in pursuit of. Are you able to find a way to flip the experience into a productive one? Can you leverage your envy into a mentorship with someone who may be able to provide excellent guidance?

Are you one of the millions of Americans that spend billions of hours per year attached to their electronic devices mindlessly scrolling on websites like Twitter, Facebook, and Instagram? Recognize the amount of time you are spending on these websites is not the only time that is not being utilized in pursuit of your life goals, but it also has an inverse relationship with your mental and physical health as it contributes to stress. Kick social media discipline drains to the curb by limiting yourself by using any number of apps that block certain sites during specific times of the day or after a specific number of minutes so you can engage in the mindless surfing within a controlled window.

Recognize that the best way to kick overwhelm to the curb is to dissect each major goal down into several sub-goals. This way, you are able to build on your momentum as you complete each task and avoid the overwhelm that can happen when you view an enormous task all at once. A little structure can go a long way in a scenario like this!

Check your perspective and be prepared to reframe and shift where you need to. Are you viewing your goals as being a sprint that must be accomplished immediately or are your viewing your goals as a marathon? If you can view your major goal pursuits as being more marathon than a sprint, you will be better prepared to endure the challenges that will arise along the road without feeling overly discouraged and ready to give up.

Be aware of your tendencies towards negative emotional reactions such as worry, because these have very real mental and physical effects. It is no good to spend so much time hyper-focusing on negative emotional states when you could instead be cultivating the self-control and willpower to move out of those negative emotional states at will. All it takes is practice, but this will be very difficult to do if you compromise your mental and physical states right out of the gate with these negative emotional states.

Diagnosing your discipline drains will go a long way towards providing you with the best framework as you work to develop and strengthen your self-discipline skills of willpower, mental toughness, and self-control.

Chapter 5: How to Flex Your "Uncomfortable Muscle"

Think for a moment; how does weight training and conditioning work for a bodybuilder? A person cannot sit on the couch and passively watch a television screen and expect to build up their muscles. In this same way, we cannot expect to be able to build the necessary muscles required for self-control, mental toughness, willpower, and self-discipline by passively waiting around for them to build themselves.

In fact, just as a weight lifter must continually reinforce their muscle's abilities to lift varying amounts of weight, a person looking to build their self-discipline muscle must also work it out regularly. Muscles must be used and stretched beyond their comfort zone, and that is what the practice of flexing your "uncomfortable muscle" will do.

Mental toughness also requires the ability to be physically tough. Interestingly enough, this physical toughness has absolutely nothing to do with physical strength levels or the size of a person's biceps or quads. This physical toughness that is being referred to is the ability to be uncomfortable and sit in the discomfort of life, and it is directly proportional to the amount of mental toughness a person has cultivated.

Just as the Navy SEALS are trained under severe and extraordinary circumstances in order to push them to their extreme stress limits, it is important for a person looking to develop their self-discipline skills to build their mental toughness by allowing themselves to become accustomed to sitting in the discomfort of the moment, whatever it may be. Any new venture in life will likely require some discomfort as it will stretch you beyond what you have done before, but it is in this stretching that growth and progress are made. Just as a muscle can only grow through being worked out, so too is it that the only way that a person's ability to grow is to essentially be worked out, or tried and tested.

All too often, people fear this process or stop just short of pushing themselves to the point of discomfort. The discomfort of life is where all of the new growth of improvement lies, so this is of utmost importance. People are extraordinarily resilient and can typically take on so much more than what they imagine they are capable of, but we hear conflicting messages throughout our lives that make us second guess this capability. Children are taught to be careful, watch out, and avoid getting hurt. The message being given to them here is to use caution in what they do because getting hurt and being in pain and experiencing discomfort is the thing they must avoid at all costs. If a child does get hurt, well-meaning caregivers rush to remove the pain by distracting them with silly songs, jokes, kisses, and Band-Aids. Of course, it would never be suggested that a caregiver should not be watching out for their children's safety or be there to comfort them and help them bandage up their scrapes, but it would probably do the childless of a disservice if the overriding message didn't seem to be one of pity and fear.

Discomfort and pain are normal parts of life, and the ability to endure them in pursuit of a goal is crucial to reaching high levels of success and achievement. In fact, studies have shown that the higher amount of "grit" that a person has, or the amount of perseverance and determination they have to sit with the discomfort and pain of whatever they need to complete to reach their goals, the more likely they are to have higher GPA scores than their peers with similar IQ's and education levels and opportunities and are more likely to be successful in high-stress competitive scenarios such as the National Spelling Bee and the West Point cadet training academy.

People who display high levels of grit often also have higher levels of self-control, meaning that they are able to better control their actions to continue to persevere in the pursuit of their goal better than their peers. One of the most interesting aspects of the studies on the grit characteristic is that intelligence and access to resources doing not seem to matter to their level of success. Just as with self-discipline, it is not about how smart a person is or how advantageous their environment is; the true determiner of how successful a person will be in their achievement lies in their self-control and self-discipline to persevere through the tough times and obstacles to reach their goals.

This is why mental toughness is so incredibly important to cultivate! Luckily, this is a skill that can be built and developed with repetition and consistency. To begin, take stock of your current mental toughness aptitude. Think back to the last time you felt very uncomfortable. This can be physical or mental discomfort. Perhaps you had to use the restroom and had to wait for the space to open up. Remember what your thoughts were. Were they panic style thoughts, "ahhhh what is taking so long??? They need to hurry up before I have an accident! This is ridiculous!" or were you able to mentally acknowledge that you were waiting and there would be nothing more to do but wait until space freed up, so you thought of other things rather than hyper-focusing on the discomfort you were experiencing?

Or perhaps your last truly uncomfortable experience was mental. For example, it can be very uncomfortable to have to meet someone important for the first time, maybe someone you work with or work for, someone you admire greatly and want to make a great first impression with. During the normal nervousness that can happen before and during important meetings like this, some people go to a lot of internal negative self-talk whereby they criticize and second guess themselves, and may end up flying through the meeting with little to no present awareness of what they are doing as they are simply focusing on "getting through it." Others are able to steady themselves and calm their nerves and remain present at the moment and the meeting, truly listening to the words the other person is saying and responding authentically.

It can also be helpful to create a list of the five most uncomfortable experiences you've ever had in your life, and this can include both uncomfortable mental/social/psychological situations and physical/medical situations. Creating a list allows you to look honestly at the situations that cause you discomfort so you can understand how to build your mental toughness in those areas. One of the most effective ways to flip the script on a lack of mental toughness is to give your brain dress rehearsals of the scenarios that cause discomfort. The importance here is on using visualization to essentially trick the brain into believing you are actually living through and experiencing the discomfort. Interestingly, in brain scans, it can be seen that the exact same areas of the brain are active while imagining something happening and while actually doing the thing, so essentially your brain does not know the difference between imagination and reality!

Visualization of the scenarios that have caused you discomfort before give you the opportunity to change the story. Rather than the negative panic style self-talk that you may be engaged in during a situation of discomfort, instead shift the inner dialogue into positive motivations. Rather than, "I have no idea why I'm here or what I'm doing here. This is terrifying!" switch it to something likes, "I love that I'm here and doing this, this is going to be great!" There has also been some recent research indicating that internal self-talk directed in a second person format such, "You love that you're here and what you're doing here, this is going to be great!" is even more effective at bolstering self-confidence and convincing our brains that we are doing well. Either way, the emphasis must be on changing the story from one in which the discomfort you encountered caused you to double down in it to a story in which you can acknowledge the discomfort but direct your mind to think of something else or to work to motivate you to survive through the discomfort by using the positive self-talk script from above. The more of this visualization dress rehearsal/walk through you complete, the better prepared you will be when you encounter the situation in the real world.

There are also many simple but effective ways to increase your mental toughness by challenging yourself in physical ways designed to test your ability to withstand discomfort. The first of which is as simple as a cold shower! Research suggests that even just letting the shower run cold for the last 30 seconds of your shower gives you an opportunity to practice sitting in discomfort. As your body reacts to the water turning colder and colder, you have an excellent opportunity to practice the positive self-talk that can keep you focused and moving through it. It could perhaps sound something like this, "Okay, water is getting colder, but that's okay, you're doing great! Getting a little colder, very bracing, but you can do it. Very, very, cold, but it's okay. It's only 30 seconds. Anyone can do anything for only 30 seconds. You've got this!"

Note the time acknowledgment at the end. Some people find it very helpful to have a reminder of the expected amount of time that they will be sitting with the discomfort. Some people really like having countdown clocks and alarms counting down to when their discomfort will end. This phenomenon is likely due to the fact that while using self-control and willpower, having an idea about how long you will need to be engaging yours for will allow you to continue to push through past exhaustion if you are able to recognize that there is "only" so much time left. It is what can keep overworked grad students trudging through their last semester as they are overloaded, overworked, and under-rested, but they recognize and understand that there is "only" so much time left and know they can continue to push themselves because there is an end in sight; this is the proverbial light at the end of the tunnel. There are many scenarios in which this may be all that is necessary to motivate someone to continue to work hard to reach their goal.

Another relatively simple way to push your limits physically and flex your uncomfortable muscle is to push your workout. There are a variety of ways to do this. Even if you are a person who does not regularly work out, you can easily utilize this exercise as well. It as simple as deciding on an exercise of your choosing: sit-ups, push-ups, jogging, lifting weights, whatever works for you. Begin the exercise as you normally would, but while you are doing the exercises, pay close attention to your mental processes. You want to practice controlling your thoughts and your internal and external responses to the discomfort you are experiencing, so take special care to stay in the moment. Notice as your discomfort grows; resist the urge to stop and instead rewire the response your brain is having to the discomfort.

For example, if you chose sit-ups as your choice for this exercise, it may feel natural for your brain to begin complaining of the pain you are experiencing in your abdomen and the sweat that is gathering on your brow. Maybe this is the norm: "Ugh, this is killing my abs. I feel so sweaty; this is gross. I'm so done." Instead of doubling down on the discomfort and describing the things you don't like, work instead to shift your perspective to a positive. It may sound something like this, "Oh wow, this is really working my abs. I can feel that sweat forming; I must really be getting an incredible workout! I'm so happy I'm getting this awesome workout, I'm going to have such tight abs after this!"

The more you can shift your mindset from one of self-pity to one of self-celebration or focus on the end result of your efforts and discomfort, the more successful you will be in persevering through the difficult moments in life, both mental and physical.

There is an exercise that the ancient Stoic philosopher Cato did often in his daily life that built incredible mental toughness and put his mental state into what he considered to be a proper perspective. Cato would wear a color tunic that was horribly out of fashion and walk through the streets barefoot, both of which were major fashion mistakes that exposed him to fashion criticism and judgment from his peers. The reason he did this was so that he could get used to the discomfort of criticism and judgment and be able to shift his perspective from one in which he worried about the judgment about others to one in which it did not bother him anymore.

Allowing yourself to experience and be exposed to uncomfortable situations and experiences gives your mind and body the experience to undergo discomfort and realize that while a situation may be difficult to live through, you will be okay on the other end of it. Doing this regularly helps to disconnect and desensitize the connections that we have between discomfort and danger and/or panic. Feeling uncomfortable is not only okay, but it is also necessary when a person is trying something new, learning something new or challenging, or really pursuing any significant goal that requires time, effort, and hard work.

Just as a bodybuilder must lift weights and work out their body to increase their strength, a person who wants to build and strengthen their mental toughness and grit must also do things that push their current limits and allow them to grow. Building that mental toughness by flexing your uncomfortable muscle is an essential piece of the puzzle when developing your self-discipline skills.

Chapter 6: How to Create a More Disciplined Environment for Yourself

In everything a person does in life, it is important to do what you are able to try to arrange the circumstances and environment you are in to contribute the most to success. A successful environment for a person who is looking to cultivate stronger self-discipline skills in their life should be one that makes staying focused on the task at hand a fairly painless choice. Most people would not dream of setting up an office space in the middle of an amusement park, right? You would never get anything done!

To begin, it will depend on where you are and what your goals are as to what the specifics of your environment restructuring will be. However, there are some fairly easy generalized tweaks that can be made to most people's environment.

For example, most people will find that electronic distractions occur often and throw us out of our focused mindset, and this is true almost universally across the board whether you are a landscaper working outside, a fitness trainer at the gym, an entrepreneur working from home, or a teacher's assistant in a conventional classroom. The single most distracting device that we all- or almost all of us- have and carry around directly on our person day in and day out is our cell phone. Pretty much everyone over the age of 10 has their own cell phone, and most of them are smartphones that have constant access to the internet and capability to conduct our banking business, check emails, watch movies, listen to music, connect via social media, get news updates, and of course-communicate with others via call and text functions. As wonderful as it is to have all of this at the tips of our fingers, the unfortunate reality is that having this sort of all in one constant entertainment and connectivity device is a major productivity killer and often an obstacle in a person's self-discipline struggle.

While trying to build self-discipline skills, the last thing that anyone needs is the ultimate distraction tool in their pockets. The pull and temptation of the smartphone on most of us is just too great, and it is a simple enough endeavor to just remove this distraction tool from our physical reach entirely while we are in the middle of a goal pursuit that requires focused attention. For some people, this may mean leaving their cell phone in their car, tucking it away in a desk drawer, charging it in another room away from they're working, or even turning it off during their working hours. There are apps available that will restrict functions of your smartphone depending on the time of the day to assist you in fighting the temptation to mindlessly scroll or take unplanned breaks from your work. This is one of those times that you really know yourself best and have to make the choice of what will work best for you.

No one wants to have to fight to keep on task, so building an environment that supports and facilitates self-discipline is crucial to supporting yourself in this endeavor. For many entrepreneurs and work from home employees, staying on a work task from the comfort of their own home can be exceptionally difficult. An important aspect here is in mindset. A person working from home must not accept the idea that working from home means you can roll out of bed anytime you want and shuffle around the house in their pajamas and then eventually at some point get to their work and they will be successful and productive because this is not true. A person working from home must almost work harder than those working at a distinct physical location because they are fighting against productivity and successes great enemy: complacency. It is too easy to become complacent and sit sipping our coffee and gazing out the window when there is no one physically around to hold us accountable for our actions. In order to avoid that, there are specific steps that work from home people can make.

To begin, there needs to be a structured and planned routine. It does not matter when you decide that you will begin work for the day, but you must have a beginning and an end. Without these two formal time markers, you run the risk of spending a day where your self-control and willpower become tapped out just trying to get yourself back on task and figure out what else you will need to do before you break for the day. If you instead schedule yourself for an opening and closing time, including breaks and lunch break, you can take all of the mental guesswork out of this and instead spend your time working just focusing on the work and the time on break just relaxing on your break. Otherwise, it is too common to allow breaks to stretch minutes and even sometimes hours beyond what they should or to allow whole days go by where not much-structured work was completed and when you review your day, you have to wonder what on earth you did all day.

This is where setting alarms can be very helpful. Set the alarm to wake up in the morning, set the alarm to get to work, set the alarm to take your first break, set the alarm to signal the end of the break, and so on. This is important because you are building the structure that you can easily follow and save all the mental guesswork for your focus and willpower. Don't tap your self-discipline energy by trying to summon the willpower to make yourself return to work. Just tell yourself that when the alarm goes off, it is time to get back to work. No questions asked, it simply is what it is. It will relieve you of that mental burden.

In addition to having a structured routine, there must also be a structured space and a structured atmosphere. It will be easier to sit down and focus on the task at hand if you feel as if you are showing up for work rather than loafing around your apartment in your bathrobe. It will also be more difficult to sit down and execute difficult tasks in the comfortable leather recliner versus having a dedicated workspace that is set up for your work and your work only. Some people that work from home also like to make signage to hang on their door that indicates they are holding work hours inside so if they do encounter any unexpected visits from friends, it is clear from the beginning that they are working inside and cannot host an impromptu afternoon coffee date. This is also something that will build on itself. If you have traditionally been the type of person that friends and colleagues could easily pull away for an afternoon coffee, then there will be a bit of an adjustment time as word gets around that you are no longer able to engage in this sort of spontaneous downtime. After a while of asserting your new priorities and plans, the people around you will come to understand that you are going to stay consistent with them.

There are other minor tweaks that can be made that can also help to better facilitate an optimum environment for self-discipline, including allowing ensuring your workspace is adequately lit. Research has shown that a well-lit environment decreases eye strain and fatigue, and in particular, it has been found that natural light encourages productivity by improving mood, increasing alertness, and decreasing stress. It is also suggested that floor lamps can be a better choice for darker workspaces as they can be more easily adjusted to avoid glare on screens and to better concentrate the light where you need it.

In addition to adequate lighting, it is important to also ensure that your workspace has ergonomic features designed to ensure you can work the stretches of time required to reach your goals without becoming quickly fatigued. If the chair you have chosen to do your work in is not ergonomic or does not promote a good sitting posture, you will find that you end up needing to take frequent breaks to relieve your spine of the stress of the poor sitting posture, and you can even find that you end up with longer-lasting back pain that keeps you from being able to sit in your workspace for long stretches of time. While it is always a good idea to get up and move around every so often to get your body going and reenergize yourself, you shouldn't have a chair that is injuring you!

Adjustable desk chairs are ideal so they can be adjusted to individual fit. The following are the guidelines for a healthy, ergonomic fit: 1) The screen of your laptop or desktop should be even with your eyes while seated. This is to ensure that you do not have to bend or brook your neck in order to do your work. 2) Thighs should be parallel to the floor and feet are flat on the floor in order to maintain optimum stability. 3) Your chair should ideally feature lumbar support in order to prevent slouching down in your seat.

If you'd like to upgrade your ergonomic environment even further, consider upgrading to a standing desk set up. There has been researching was done that has found associations of converting a traditional sitting desk workspace to a stand-up desk set up to increased productivity. In fact, there are even sit and stand combination desks available now, so there is an option to easily switch between sitting and standing during the course of a workday.

In cultivating an environment that is supportive of self-discipline to complete your goals, it is also important to keep the environment organized. Clutter in the workspace can contribute to distraction as you will have to search about for items you are looking for and it can even provide an impetus for procrastination if you find yourself putting off your work because you have to cut through the clutter on your desk. To avoid this, set up an organized environment from the outset. You can use a desktop organizer or a filing system to keep loose paperwork from taking over your space. Be sure to keep anything you need within easy reach as you don't want any excuses to have to get up and go wandering about looking for something you need like a stapler, scratch paper, and spare pens, whatever it may be. The more you prepare, the less likely you are to be interrupted later by your lack of preparation.

Preparing your environment to facilitate optimal self-discipline can involve restructuring your workspace, your work time, and decreasing common distractions to productivity such as clutter and lack of preparation. It is important when you are building the self-discipline skills that you set yourself up for success as best as you can. An ounce of prevention is worth a pound of the cure, especially when it comes to distractions that can easily undermine your self-discipline efforts.

Chapter 7: The Relationship You Need to Build with Willpower

In any endeavor you choose to undertake in this life, there will be a necessity to build and utilize a relationship with one crucial skill in particular. This skill is willpower. Willpower is your ability to use your strength to overcome short-term desires or temptations to achieve your long-term goals. There are many, many ways to describe this very important skill, but there is one thing that is for sure and for certain. Willpower is using your effort to get what you really want as an end result out of a situation rather than what you really want at the moment, and this is strikingly difficult for many.

One very common event that occurs for many people that exemplifies what happens when a person underutilizes their willpower is procrastination. In fact, about twenty percent of the population identify themselves as procrastinators, and researchers think even more people are guilty of consistently procrastinating completing tasks, from very large pursuits to small. Incredibly, among students, that number leaps to between eighty-five to ninety-five percent! This includes students from all levels of academia, including undergrad and graduate-level university students. For procrastinating students, this, unfortunately, correlates with higher levels of self-reported stress, the higher rate of illness, and lower grades.

Doesn't sound much like the path to success includes procrastination, does it?

Procrastination acts as the inverse or the opposite, of willpower. Willpower is doing what must be done at the moment, even if it comes with a pain point or current "cost," in order to gain in the long-term and reach a goal, and procrastination is putting off what must be done at the moment, pushing the pain point or "cost" further down the road; it decreases the present pain point or "cost" by transferring it to the future, often setting up for a loss in the long-term and a failure to reach the goal. By better understanding this inverse of willpower, you can more easily understand how to flip it around and strengthen your willpower.

Most procrastination occurs as a result of a feeling or impulse to avoid some form of pain or discomfort. For example, students may procrastinate writing a ten-page essay because they know it will be mentally taxing, or a business executive may procrastinate and put off filling out tedious paperwork because they know it will be boring and uninteresting.

Looking back at the work we've done around how to cultivate mental toughness, this is a perfect example of why that work is so important in building the self-discipline skills you need to be successful in your endeavors. In order to kick procrastination to the curb, you have to be willing to flex your uncomfortable muscle and sit in the discomfort of whatever the situation is you may have wanted to procrastinate in.

You can practice flexing your uncomfortable muscle to override your procrastination impulses by engaging in a fruitful internal dialogue with yourself. For example, say you come home from work every day at five o'clock to feed the cat, and then lo and behold, instead of heading out for a quick jog as you always plan to do, you instead find other things to do that you suddenly feel really must be done before your jog. Maybe you tell yourself you really ought to go ahead and clean the litter box next, or maybe you remember that your sister called you earlier in the day and you really should go ahead and call her back right now, but whatever it is that you are putting in front of your goal- in this case, your evening jog- is acting as a procrastination obstacle and you need to get a handle on that, because most people will use those obstacles as a convenient roadblock to their goal- "oops, looks like it is too late to head out for my jog now!"

You can structure an effective internal dialogue with yourself by practicing the sequence of events ahead of time in your mind. Maybe on your drive home you can visualize yourself walking in your front door, tossing your keys on the entryway table, bending over to pet the top of your cat's head while telling him that you will feed him quickly before your jog, and then continue talking about heading out for the jog as you go through the motions. Narrating your own actions can help you feel as if you are being monitored by someone else and will be accountable for your procrastination if you let other things get in the way of your procrastination. While you are narrating your actions, keep your tone, and verbiage light and upbeat. You will motivate yourself to complete the tasks you need to complete if you are talking about them as if they are not a terrible chore to be avoided.

Willpower is the ability to flip that switch from one of avoidance of the pain points of life to one in which you willingly embrace them. The relationship you have to your willpower will be very integral in how effective you are with it. If you view your willpower as something that is weak or must be fought with, then you are essentially setting yourself up for failure. If you believe your willpower is weak, then you believe you have an inefficient tool for your projects. If you believe your willpower is your enemy, then you will be wasting valuable energy and resources in "fighting" this enemy.

To reframe and revamp your relationship to willpower, you will need to shift the way you think of it. Instead of viewing it as something that must be pitied or fought, instead, view it as something that must be tended to carefully. Imagine your willpower as a seed you've just planted in your garden. You wouldn't dig a hole, place the seed in, cover it, and then start complaining how nothing has happened, right? Of course not! You would understand that you had completed an important step in planting the seed, but now you must continue to ensure that your seed has the right environment in which to grow and thrive. Your seed will not grow if it does not get enough water, nor will it grow if it gets too much. Your seed must be cared for and paid attention to.

Just as your seed requires your care and attention, so does your willpower. You have to set yourself up for success using tools such as the visualization and self-talk above. It is important that your relationship with your willpower is healthy and strong. You will not build this skill by shouting at yourself to complete a task or by hoping to "wing it." Willpower is a muscle that must be built with repetition and consistency, and as you continue to work on your muscle, it will grow and become stronger. Throughout this process, it will be easier to rely on this muscle to do this important work, but until then, you will need to continue to work on it in ways that support it and you.

Your relationship with your willpower should not be a battle. It should be a partnership, and it will require your careful attention and respect. Continue to cultivate and care for this relationship throughout your life and remember to set yourself up for success by protecting against procrastination and instead of using the tools of visualization and positive self-talk to keep your willpower seed well-watered and well-fed. Eventually, this seed will grow, and your willpower muscles will be strong enough to carry you through on the important tasks you have as you continue to reach for your goals.

Willpower is the power to do the things you must do in order to reach your dreams. Don't let this relationship falter.

Chapter 8: Eat Your Vegetables! No, Really.

You already know, "you are what you eat," right? But did you know that what you eat will actually have a direct effect on how focused and effective you are in your actions and endeavors, and this includes your willpower, your mental toughness, and your self-control, so eating your vegetables- and lots of other healthy foods- will help you in your quest to build a better self-discipline skill set.

In a very simplistic way, the foods that we put into our bodies will either work synergistically with our digestive system to pull all of the nutritive elements such as vitamins, minerals, proteins, good fats, etc. out of the foods we ingest and allow it to be absorbed into our bodies while filtering out whatever the waste products will be, or the foods that we put into our bodies will cause a lot of extra work for our digestive system, and we will end up going into what is jokingly referred to by many as a "food coma." When this happens, and our digestive system is overtaxed by what we have eaten, we feel tired, slow, lethargic, and sometimes even feel sick to our stomachs. There is a direct link between physical and mental health, and while feeling poorly, our minds are not at their sharpest, and the sharper our minds are, the more disciplined we can be. We will never be able to distinguish ourselves in a positive way from others if we are slumped over on the couch in a food coma!

One of the main culprits behind the dreaded food coma is the carbohydrate. Carbohydrates are not intrinsically unhealthy, but the way most people ingest them is. Carbohydrates are typically found in heavily processed bread and sugary type of foods, especially in what is known as a convenience food, or the stuff that is cheap and easily accessible to grab off of the shelf at the gas station while filling up! Foods like this that are very heavy in carbs typically cause a sudden and dramatic increase of insulin, the hormone that is necessary for breaking down the sugar in the foods we eat. A diabetic is unable to produce the amounts of insulin they need to adequately break this sugar down and must supplement with insulin from an external source. For people without diabetes, the body has to kick out a significant amount of insulin to break down the highly processed carbohydrates that are often over-ingested, and this has a direct effect on alertness. Sleep hormones such as tryptophan and serotonin are released in the brain from this insulin flood. This is obviously not a high-productivity, high-alert state and does not contribute to a person being able to function at the top of their game.

However, just as it is no good for our brains to be flooded with an excess of insulin that is attempting to cope with a heavy carb-laden meal, going without food for too long creates an internal environment of low blood sugar; the level of "blood sugar" refers to the glucose levels in our bodies. Research has found that glucose is what gives energy for almost all of the brain's processes, and it is thought that self-control is particularly dependent on these glucose levels! Basically, it is not an optimum internal environment for self-discipline when you either over-eat or under-eat, so the happy medium is the way to go!

There is even a burgeoning new field in healthcare referred to as nutritional psychiatry. Nutritional psychiatry emphasizes the connection between a person's food choices and their mental health. Of particular importance is the relationship between what a person consumes and the levels of and variety of bacteria that lives in the gut. The bacteria that is found in the gut is incredibly important to mood and mental health because there are neural pathways that run directly between the gut and the brain, and the foods that people ingest either contribute to the health and proliferation of the so-called "good bacteria" or the health and proliferation of the so-called "bad bacteria," and there is an optimum balance between the two that creates the best environment for gut and mental health.

In fact, research has shown that when people take a supplement that contains the "good" bacteria, referred to as probiotics, there is a decrease in anxiety levels, in their perception of stress, and an overall increase in mood and mental health outlook. It is well known that traditional diets of different cultures around the world are associated with a variety of different health outcomes, and in many of the diets that are associated with the better physical and mental health outcomes, people consume fermented foods as a regular staple of their diet. Fermenting food is a natural way to preserve otherwise easily perishable foods such as vegetables, meats, and dairy products, and fermented foods act as natural probiotics! Example of fermented foods includes sauerkraut, kimchi, and pickles. Many people choose to supplement their probiotics over ingesting fermented foods, and that's fine too! Whatever way you choose, adding probiotics to your diet is a good choice to enhance your mental strength and focus.

There are three superstar vitamins that are crucial to optimum brain function and that are integral to willpower, mental toughness, and self-control, and they are the B group vitamins, Vitamin D, and omega 3 fatty acids.

The first is the B vitamin group and B vitamin supplements typically include B1- thiamine, B2- riboflavin, B3- niacin, B5- pantothenic acid, B6- pyridoxine, B7- biotin, B9- folic acid, and B12- cobalamin. In addition to the physical effects of the deficiency of these B vitamins, there are very real mental and mood effects associated with each as well. B1 deficiency is associated with short-term memory loss and irritability. B3 deficiency is associated with depression and fatigue. B5 deficiency is associated with depression, fatigue, insomnia, and irritability. B6 deficiency is associated with depression, difficulty concentrating, irritability, nervousness, and short-term memory loss. B9 deficiency is associated with forgetfulness and irritability. B12 deficiency is associated with fatigue and weakness.

Many of these B group vitamins play an important role in regulating neurotransmitters, or the brain cells responsible for communication between the brain and our bodies. Ensuring that you have optimal levels of B group vitamins means that you will be able to more easily build the willpower, mental toughness, and self-control skills you need to build as you develop your self-discipline skill set. Some people choose to supplement their B vitamin group, but if you eat a nutritious diet, you can get all the B vitamins you need directly from the foods you eat. See the chart below for a list of B vitamin foods.

FOODS RICH IN B VITAMINS
Eggs and dairy products such as milk and cheese
Legumes such as beans and lentils
Seeds and nuts such as almonds, walnuts, and sunflower seeds
Dark, leafy greens such as spinach, kale, and broccoli
Fruits such as bananas, citrus fruits, and avocados
Whole grains such as barley, millet, and brown rice
Meat such as poultry and red meat
Fish such as trout, tuna, and salmon

If you suspect that you might not be getting all of the B vitamins you need out of your diet, talk to your doctor about how to determine if supplementation is right for you.

Next on the list of important vitamins for optimum brain function is vitamin D. Vitamin D is often referred to as the Sunshine Vitamin because it is made in our bodies when we are exposed to direct sunlight. Unfortunately, sunblock does inhibit this process, so there is a delicate balance that people must make between protecting themselves from the dangerous exposure to the sun's ultraviolet rays that can cause sunburn and skin damage and allowing enough sun exposure to adequately synthesize vitamin D internally. This is one of the reasons why we do find vitamin D added to foods such as milk and breakfast cereals.

It is known by scientists and medical professionals that vitamin D deficiencies are associated with cognitive impairment, and this is often one of the first warning signs of conditions such as Alzheimer's disease and dementia, so vitamin D supplementation has become a more frequent focus for study. It is currently believed that either two to three times week of 15-30 minute windows of direct sun exposure or supplementation between 1,000- 2,000 IU of synthetic vitamin D is probably an ideal amount for healthy vitamin D levels in the average adult. Also, keep in mind that lighter-skinned people will require less time being directly exposed to sunlight than darker-skinned people as the more melanin in your skin; the longer it takes to absorb the required amount of sunlight to manufacture vitamin D.

See the chart below for a list of foods that contain vitamin D.

FOODS THAT CONTAIN VITAMIN D
Fortified milk and milk products, such as yogurt
Eggs (higher vitamin D levels found in free-range eggs than caged eggs)
Fortified cereals
Fortified breakfast bars
Fish such as tuna and salmon

If you feel that you may not be getting all the vitamin D you need from the sun and your diet, speak to your health professional to see if vitamin D supplementation might be right for you.

The final nutrient on the list is considered essential to the health and activity of the brain and is a potent anti-inflammatory. Omega 3 fatty acids are important fats that are crucial for a healthy brain, particularly in the early development stages of life. Omega 3 fatty acids consist of EPA and DHA, which both are very important for the health and maintenance of brain functions throughout a person's lifetime. In fact, blood tests in older adults revealed that lower levels of DHA are associated with a sign of aging in the brain- smaller brain size.

In order to prevent any deficits in this important component of brain function, particularly for most people who follow a typical western diet that does not include significant amounts of omega 3 fatty acids' best food sources such as nuts, seeds, and fish, some people choose to supplement.

The chart below has a list of omega 3 fatty acid-rich food sources.

FOODS RICH IN OMEGA 3 FATTY ACIDS
Fish such as salmon, trout, mackerel, anchovies, tuna, and sardines
Dark green leafy vegetables such as kale, spinach, and Brussels sprouts
Seaweed, spirulina, chlorella, and nori
Seeds such as flaxseeds, chia seeds, and hemp seeds
Nuts such as walnuts, butternuts, and cashews
Beans such as kidney beans and edamame
Soybean oil

If you think that you may not be getting the amount of omega 3 fatty acid that you need in your daily diet, speak to your healthcare practitioner about supplementation.

An important aspect of health that most people are very well aware of is hydration, particularly with water. But did you know that water is incredibly important to how your brain functions? Water should be thought of as another important nutrient, particularly when it comes to brain health.

Drinking adequate amounts of water and remaining properly hydrated is associated with a strong memory, concentration, and cognition, and it has a positive effect on mood and emotions as well. A part of this is because drinking water increases blood flow and oxygen to the brain.

Studies have shown that even mild hydration can impair concentration and mood. Water is incredibly important to health and well-being, and its role in brain function means it must be a part of your nutritional strategy of supporting your brain to its optimal levels so you can continue to build on the necessary skills of self-discipline. Experts suggest that people drink about half a gallon of water per day.

In order to better develop the necessary skills of self-discipline such as willpower, mental toughness, and self-control, it is important that the brain (and body!) are functioning at optimal levels. What we put into our bodies matters, and nutrition is a great way to ensure that we have set ourselves up for success, whatever our endeavors may be.

Remember to eat moderately, support your gut, get plenty of the brain-boosting vitamins and minerals such as the B group vitamins, vitamin D, and omega 3 fatty acids, and drink plenty of water. You will need all the brainpower you can muster as you work to develop your self-discipline skills!

Part 3: Self-Discipline Strategies

Self-discipline strategies are going to be the specific strategies you use as you work to put all of the theories and practices together that have been covered in the first two parts of this book. A strategy is a plan of action, and that is exactly what you will receive. Chapter 9 will explain how your mindset and how you approach both the development of your self-discipline skills and any other endeavor in life will set the tone for either success or failure, and how it can directly affect your happiness and fulfillment in life. Chapter 10 will provide you with the quick fix guide that you can refer back to in moments of "crisis" when you find your self-discipline slipping, Chapter 11 will outline additional strategies for success, and Chapter 12 will provide a summary guide of the material that has been covered here that you can refer back to anytime you need to brush back up on some of the key tenets of this book.

Self-discipline is a practice. It is not a characteristic that a person either has or does not have. It is a set of skills that must be worked on and developed, just as any other skills must be. Some people will find these skills easier to acquire than others, and some people will find these skills easier to put into real-world practice than others. That does not matter; all that matters is that you develop the self-discipline strategies that will work for you in your life.

Self-discipline is more than a theory. Everyone will have to tailor this information to fit into their own personal circumstances, and even that will be an exercise in self-discipline. You are almost to the end of this book, but you are just beginning on this journey towards greater self-discipline. Stay focused and keeps your eyes on your prize, whatever it may be! You deserve it.

Chapter 9: Why Your Mindset and Approach Are Everything

Did you know that how you view yourself and the work you do can be the make or break difference in your success level in almost any endeavor? This is absolutely the case, and how you feel and what you believe about yourself including your ability to grow, learn, and achieve, will determine how likely it is for you to reach your goals.

There are two different mindsets that people typically fall into: The first is a fixed mindset, and a person with a fixed mindset will believe that the qualities and characteristics they possess, such as their intelligence, their talents, their personalities, etc., were all fixed at birth and are relatively unchangeable. The second is a growth mindset, and a person with a growth mindset believes that these characteristics can all be developed and strengthened through learning and practice.

A person with a fixed mindset will tend to accept that they have limitations in certain skills that they do not possess and will avoid attempting to improve on those skills. A person with a growth mindset will understand that no one is born knowing everything! Some people may tend to have more of a natural inclination towards something, but that doesn't mean that people that do not share that same easy inclination are not capable of learning it by utilizing consistent practice. Growth mindsets result in learning and improvement.

There is some research to suggest that mindsets are developed fairly early on in life from the messages that children receive from their parents, peers, teachers, and other important people in their life. People with fixed mindsets were often taught that it is the end result rather than the process of reaching for and achieving that matters. These would be the people who are afraid of failure because they received the message somewhere along the way that they should not try to achieve things that they know they will not easily achieve. Fear of failure keeps them believing that they are as they are, and no amount of applied effort will change that.

People with growth mindsets were typically taught that the journey of discovery and achievement were just as important as the end result. These people were taught that making mistakes and failing at something is just a part of trying to achieve anything, and they often view failures as setbacks rather than catastrophes. A person with a growth mindset is the kind of person who will accept something difficult or that they are not immediately good at as a challenge and an opportunity. For example, perhaps someone plays golf for the first time and is unable to make it on the green for a single hole. Rather than find themselves wanting to avoid the experience again, they might turn around at the end of the game and suggest that they meet up at the range the following day so they can hit golf balls together. Their current status of not being able to perform the way they want to be not viewed as a problem or something to be upset about. It is a challenge, and it means there are new skills they need to work to develop!

People with a fixed mindset often like to double down on their inability to do something, such as the scenario that often plays out with someone who claims they just "aren't any good at math," and so they do whatever they can in their power to avoid it. This is an example of how sometimes people choose the path of least resistance or the thing that we know, even if it is an uncomfortable path because we are comfortable or familiar with it. In a situation such as the self-proclaimed "not good at math" person, the issue is that this provides an easy out or an easy excuse for them to not have to try. After all, why would they try to learn more math or do better when it obviously won't help; after all, they "aren't any good at math," right? Now they never really have to try because they have a convenient out.

The idea behind a growth mindset is that there is enormous potential for a human to achieve, independent of any genetic or conditional characteristics bestowed on them early on in their lives. Brains can always be strengthened and new neural pathways can be formed. Plans and goals can always be shifted as long as a person continues moving forward, and pretty much anything is possible with effort and hard work.

It is not the end result that defines you. It is the process.

Chances are that if you picked up a book such as this one, you are likely in the growth mindset category, and this is GREAT. However, even if you find yourself leaning towards the fixed mindset and struggle to believe that you are indeed capable of learning new and significant skills such as self-discipline, all is not lost because you are capable of developing more of a growth mindset.

What's more, there is a large payoff for doing so. Research suggests that there are many advantages that are associated with having a growth mindset. People with a growth mindset have more prosocial behaviors, less anxiety, less aggression, higher self-esteem, higher levels of "grit" and mental toughness, and better self-regulation.

In an academic setting, the differences between students with a fixed mindset and the students with a growth mindset were significant. When teachers praised children for their efforts rather than their intelligence (remarks such as "You worked really hard on that!" vs. "You are so smart!") the students were more likely to pursue future projects that would help them learn something new, vs. the children praised for their intelligence that would more often only choose projects they felt comfortable completing well, indicating that it was important to them to retain the label of "smart." In doing so, those children are learning to play it safe rather than to work hard and do their best.

Also, children who were being praised for their intelligence reported less enjoyment from the stated tasks than the children who were praised for their effort. Children praised for their intelligence were also less likely to complete difficult tasks, and the children praised for their effort were more likely to persist.

Children who had been praised for their intelligence actually found themselves performing worse over time, whereas the children who had been praised for their efforts increasingly performed better and better.

A very interesting side-effect of this praise of intelligence vs. process was that the children praised for their intelligence requested information about how the other children performed at about a rate of 86%, whereas the children praised for their effort only asked for this similar information at a rate of about 13%. This is a HUGE difference!

This difference transfers to employees in traditional business setups as well. Employees at companies that employ traditional fixed mindset techniques such as a focus on end result and static talent report being more worried about failure and so they regularly take "safe" routes, squashing innovation in their industry. There is also an unfortunate tendency of employees in fixed-mindset companies to find ways to cut corners and stay ahead in order to remain considered a valuable asset at their company.

Compare this to companies such as Microsoft that have mindfully created a growth mindset culture amongst their employees by encouraging development and innovation by focusing on the process rather than the result. One of the programs they engage in is to have "hackathons" where employees spend a day in collaboration to create a new "hack" and even go so far as to develop it via a business plan, a prototype, and a company-wide pitch.

This sort of conscious engineering into steering innovation by focusing on process has huge payoffs as employees are willing to put themselves out there and push their own boundaries when they feel as though this will be valued regardless of if the end product is a success in and of itself. Microsoft hit a home run with this exercise when a hackathon team created the Learning Tools for OneNote!

Companies that employ an active growth mindset approach for their employees have found that not only do their employees work more transparently because they are less afraid of making "mistakes" or encountering setbacks, they also are better at embodying a spirit of teamwork where everyone is valued for their contributions. A growth mindset encourages everyone to contribute in whatever way they can without fear of being the cause of failure or disappointment for their team.

Available statistics demonstrate the difference in employee perception in workplaces that foster the growth mindset approach; employees in workplaces that foster the growth mindset approach rate their co-workers as trustworthy 47% times more than employees in workplaces that do not foster the growth mindset approach. There is also a difference in how strongly employees in workplaces that foster the growth mindset approach feel about their commitment levels, with these employees being 34% more likely to express strong commitment to their workplace organization vs. employees that do not, which means that the employees that are engaging in a growth mindset approach are more likely to put in the work and effort to see results for their company.

This is an important takeaway when considering the difference between the growth mindset and the fixed mindset. A person with a growth mindset will recognize that the process of building new skills, such as self-discipline, is an important task and outcome in and of itself. It is not the end result that matters the most, but rather the learning that comes with the process. It is not that the end itself does not matter; it is just not the entire event. A person with a fixed mindset may find themselves more willing to cut corners to get to the end and achieve whatever the end goal is and consider the process of learning to be insignificant because that is not the most important part of their quest.

People can naturally have a little bit of a growth mindset in some areas of their lives and a little bit of a fixed mindset in others, and people can further develop a growth mindset in any area of their life that they choose. If you want to develop more a growth mindset, the first step is to better understand what areas of your life you hold a fixed mindset in. Look back at your childhood. What skills did you want to learn that you then went on to learn? This could be improving at a sport or learning an instrument, or something similar. Think back to how you were as you learned your new skill. Were you excited to be learning something new? Did you approach each new lesson as a fun activity? Or were often upset that the skill required lots of repetition and struggle? Did you approach each lesson as a frustrating activity?

Now consider the different scenarios in your life when you have quit something. Maybe it was an organized activity like a class or a team or maybe even a job. What were the thought processes behind the desire to quit? Did you want to quit because it was just not coming to you as quickly as you wanted it to, or did you quit for an external reason because of a scheduling conflict or something similarly unavoidable?

These questions will help you gain insight into what kind of a mindset you have operated from in your life, and you can begin to better use this your mindset to operate your life at its highest level.

Shifting towards a growth mindset and approaching life as a process of pursuit and learning can be the difference between both successfully reaching your goals and also between having greater happiness and fulfillment in your life. A growth mindset will help to shift you towards viewing the entire process of learning, growing, and developing as a beneficial and fulfilling activity, regardless of what your past experience has been. Anyone can shift their mental mindset towards a growth mindset once they approach each goal as a process, rather than an event. The end result is not the most fulfilling part of the journey. The person you develop into during the process is the most fulfilling part.

Chapter 10: Quick Fix Guide: Read in Case of Temptation

Are you feeling like you might be losing the self-discipline to pursue the skills required for self-discipline? Are you wondering if you have what it takes to build and develop your self-control, your willpower, and your mental toughness? Are you wondering how you will ever be able to easily draw on the information you have learned in this book to follow through with any endeavor you start and distinguish yourself from others in your field?

That's okay. Everyone needs a little inspiration sometimes, and an easy to follow step-by-step guide to build and strengthen the habits of self-discipline that you have learned throughout this book.

Let's begin with the inspiration and the reminder of what self-discipline can do for a person's life. Did you ever see the 2006 film "The Pursuit of Happiness," starring Will Smith? Did you know it is based on true events? Chris Gardner, played by Will Smith in the film, was in fact in a position in life where he had very little available resources and many disadvantages working against him. Gardner invested his life savings into cutting edge medical equipment that would make him a handsome profit, but when a series of events occurs that leads to his wife moving away that leaves him a single father in charge of his very young son, his eviction from his apartment, and losing one of the medical devices that he desperately needed to turn a profit, he did not lay down and give up. Instead, he doubled down on his willpower, self-control, and mental toughness.

Chris Gardner is one of the true-life testimonials of what willpower, self-control, and mental toughness can do for a person. Gardner could have easily given up at any moment in time. His circumstances were stacked against him, but rather than decide to take the easy way out. He used his mental toughness, self-control, and willpower to persist in scenarios that would break most people. In the end, Gardner's ambitions became a reality because he did not give up. He managed to keep focused on his goal and to make each step of his plans happen even in the face of great adversity.

Gardner's story is so inspirational because he managed to take what was incredible adversity and leverage it into the stunning success of opening his own million-dollar brokerage firm. He managed to do this because he worked hard and did not let his incredible hardship break him mentally. This sort of mental toughness is inspirational to anyone looking to cultivate more of that particular quality in themselves, and his entire story is a shining example of what self-discipline can do for someone in the pursuit of their dreams.

Another highly inspirational example of someone doing incredible things through self-discipline skills is the world-renowned professional golfer, Phil Mickelson. Considered one of the best golfers of all time, he was not simply born with this kind of incredible talent and ability. He developed it through willpower, self-control, and mental toughness.

Phil Mickelson has a practice of working on his putts that is extraordinarily disciplined. It is reported that he does drills of three-foot putts, one hundred in a row. If he misses one of these hundred three-foot putts, he starts the count over! This particular practice requires the willpower, self-control, and mental toughness skills to hold himself to this practice, even after he misses a putt at putt number 98! Can you imagine the kind of willpower, self-control, and mental toughness that it must require for him to do this after he has been performing this same simple three-foot putt for hours? It's an extraordinary amount, indeed, and almost more important than the muscle memory and the talented skill that he is building by repetition is the mental focus and clarity he is building by this self-discipline practice. He is developing his self-discipline at the same time he is building his golf skill, and the two together are what makes him one of the best golfers the world has ever seen.

If you want to find your greatness, develop your ambition, and reach your goals in the same way that the Chris Gardner's and Phil Mickelson's of the world have, then you must work the steps to build your willpower, self-control, and mental toughness. Greatness is never accidental. It must be cultivated and strengthened, and this is possible by first training yourself in the self-discipline strategies that have been covered in this book.

There are steps you can take to make yourself more likely to meet your self-discipline goals. One easy step you can take is to shift your perception of what the skills of self-discipline really mean. The basic idea here is that in order to develop your practice of willpower, self-control, and mental toughness into long-lasting habits, you must rewire your brain to be able to pull from these skill sets easier.

Let's begin with what science already knows about habits and how they are built. Researchers state that habits actually can account for up to 40% of a person's behaviors in any given day! Talk about living life on autopilot, right?

The trick then becomes to develop the kinds of habits that you want to live your life by, even operating on autopilot. As was referenced earlier in this work, most of us brush our teeth on autopilot. This is a good thing! Can you imagine the kind of time that would be essentially wasted by having to consider and will yourself into completing the entire process twice a day? Thank goodness for autopilot!

One effective strategy for rewiring your brain to develop long-lasting habits is to focus on building a new identity for yourself, with identity-based habits. This necessitates not just focusing on the outcomes or the habits that you want to develop, but focusing on the person you will become. The difference here is that one is centered around what a person wants to be, and the other is centered around who a person wants to become. The best way to achieve this shift in identity is to become a person who does whatever the thing is you want to become.

For example, if your focus is on losing weight as a goal, then it may be tempting to focus on all the different mini-goals that you will need to achieve to reach your ultimate goal. Perhaps a part of this may look like going to the gym every morning and doing yoga every night. As great as those two things are to help you reach your ultimate goal, it is important that you work to shift your identity, too. You want to become not only a person who loses some weight but a person who consistently embodies the identity of a person who has a healthy weight.

For example, a person who has a healthy weight likely has a relatively healthy lifestyle. That person most likely makes healthy choices when they eat out at restaurants. This doesn't mean they order the food they hate, just that they have learned to enjoy healthier options. Now that they enjoy healthier options, they are the kind of person who orders healthier options off of restaurant menus. This is now a part of their identity, and they are no longer just dieting to lose some weight. Now they are a person with a healthy diet!

One way to ensure you can fully immerse yourself in the identity of the trait, skill, or goal that you are pursuing is to practice shifting your perspective and belief systems. Going back to the last example about a person that shifts their identity from one of a person wanting to lose weight to one of a person who has a healthy weight, developing a habit of choosing healthy foods will require some mental work.

This mental work may look something like going grocery shopping with a list of foods that are all healthy and a part of a great healthy diet and then going back home and learning three new recipes to make with these new healthy foods. While you are shopping for healthy foods, train your brain to view them differently. Instead of thoughts such as "Arugala??? What the heck does arugula even taste like, ugh," try instead to blaze a new neural path in which you associate dark leafy greens with something positive? Maybe the new script you can follow might sound something like this, "Arugula!!! Look at those colors, wow. That is a deep green and purple combination, how gorgeous. I could almost turn this into a bouquet and take a picture of it!" Then when you are packing your arugula up, you might decide to hold it in your hands for a moment before placing in your cart and allow yourself to feel gratitude and pride that you are able to buy something so healthy and vibrant for yourself. Do the same when you unpack your groceries at home. You want to build mental associations that are positive with these healthy foods, so your brain gets used to associating them with positive moments.

The practice should continue while you are preparing the new recipes, repeating the process of practicing gratitude for these vibrant, healthy foods, and allowing yourself to feel proud of yourself for buying them and preparing them. You want to be excited about your new recipes and meals! By the time the new recipe hits your plate, you want to already have a beautifully positive relationship with them. This way, once the new food hits your tongue, you are able to keep the positive associations continuing on rather than approaching the entire experience with a negative skepticism.

Now when you are in a position to make a choice between a healthy option or an unhealthy option while out at a restaurant with friends, it will be significantly easier to call on the self-discipline you will need to not fall back on old habits because you have rewired your brain to make the self-discipline easier. No one likes a fight, especially your brain, so set up your goals and pursuits so that you don't have to fight for them in a way that will wear you out and zap your willpower. It is possible to cultivate your identity and shift the way you perceive certain things to make self-discipline a more pleasant and affirming process than some find it to be.

Chapter 11: Additional Strategies for Success

Ever heard of the saying, "don't waste time trying to reinvent the wheel?" Well, this is often a good thing to remember when it comes to personal success, as there is much to learn from other's that have paved the way before you. There are well-known (and some not-so-well-known) strategies and psychological shortcuts that you can adapt for your own use, and you absolutely should!

Strategy #1: Find And Outline Your Mission

For so many people in this world, their lives exist as a day to day exercise in improvisation. For some people, this will work just fine for them and their personal goals, but for people who are destined for greatness in their industry and want to operate at the top of their field, they require a mission strategy. You might consider it almost as a personal business plan, the cultivation of the business of YOU.

You need to outline the HOW. What are the specific practices you have chosen to adopt from this work? Be specific and outline how it will look in your daily life. What are the specific daily strategies and practices that you will be used to develop and train yourself in the self-discipline specific skills that you have learned about in this book? Make yourself a daily/weekly/monthly schedule in which you are outlining the specific practices you will be making and choose a date at least 21 days in the future to check in with yourself about your progress.

Strategy #2: Find Your Why

If you proceed down your list of goals and find yourself feeling less than motivated, you might need to use the Find Your Why Strategy. You have to be clear with the WHY of what you are doing. Why are you pursuing self-discipline strategies? What parts of your life are going to be most positively affected by your newly developed skills of willpower, self-control, and mental toughness? When you find yourself feeling like you might be on the verge of losing your motivation, you have to come back to the reasons that made you begin to seek out this specific skill set in the first place.

Some people like to make out a list of their WHY that can be kept easily accessible to them. This might be a digital list kept easily accessible on all of their devices, or perhaps a physical list that is typed up, printed out, framed, and hung in the physical locations you think you might need it most. Some people like to keep their WHY lists in both their work locations, such as hanging over a desk and also in their personal locations where they might find themselves sitting with a cup of a coffee and relaxing, such as in a favorite reading chair at home. Some people like to have their WHY list where they will see it at predictable times, such as hanging next to the bathroom mirror so while they are brushing their teeth and washing their face in the morning, they will have that time to consider and contemplate their WHY.

Keeping the reasons why you are putting in the big effort at the forefront of your mind can keep you motivated and on your game regardless of how difficult things may get.

Strategy #3: Define Your Circle Of Competence

The circle of competence is a model that was developed and popularized by American billionaire Warren Buffett to describe the areas of expertise that we all have. The basic idea is that everyone has their own individual circle of competence and that this circle of competence will encompass all of the things that a person knows so well that they can be considered an expert in this area. The circle of competence model suggests that when people understand and take advantage of their circle of competence, they are able to cash in on this level of expertise. When a person tries to operate beyond their circle of competence, problems can arise.

A simplistic way to view it is this: Who do you call when your kitchen sink backs up? Do you call the grocery store up the street that you buy your milk and eggs from? Do you call the car dealership that you purchased your car from? Of course not. You would call a plumber, an expert in the area that you need the work done in. That is the plumber's circle of competence, and when you need plumbing work done, that is who you call in!

You must understand and define your own circle of competence so you can take advantage of opportunities to use your expertise. You also want to avoid situations where you overextend yourself in an area that you do not the sufficient level of competence required to complete the task successfully. If you understand your strengths and weaknesses, you can use them in the ways that will produce the greatest success for yourself.

Strategy #4: Measure Your Progress

Measuring your progress is important because you want to know how your goals are shaping up; figuring out what is working and what isn't is an important part of the process because if there is something that is not working out for you, you will need to troubleshoot it to see how it might be tweaked to work better for you. Conversely, if it seems as if progress is going well and everything is working great, then this can keep you motivated to continue on your path!

Some people like to use checklists that they set up in advance, with dates for specific goals that need to be checked off at different intervals. This provides a clear-cut methodology for measuring progress, as you either hit your goal or you did not. If an item was unable to be checked off, then you can further investigate what needs to shift in order to check that goal off.

Strategy #5: The Winner Effect

The winner effect is a phenomenon that occurs where once a person-or any animal- wins once, they are more likely to continue winning. This likely occurs because each win inspires confidence and other neurochemicals associated with happiness and ability, meaning that winners go into each new situation with this level of confidence and capability that puts them at an advantage over their competitors. Conversely, those that have a history of losing must work harder to overcome the opposite effect by prepping themselves mentally and physically to tap into the confidence and related chemical processes that aren't being produced naturally via the winner's effect. Use this knowledge to your advantage!

Strategy #6: Reward Yourself

This strategy builds upon brain science discussed earlier in this book about creating new neural pathways in the brain. By rewarding yourself when you complete something important, you are using positive reinforcement to send the message to yourself that pursuing and reaching a goal is a great thing, and each time these associations are made, the connection becomes strengthened more and more and eventually a habit of success is built.

Strategy #7: Use Commitment Devices

A commitment device is a consequence that a person commits to helping them remain committed to their plan. A true commitment device is one that is voluntarily engineered for oneself, but there is a well-known variation of it that plays out in parenting often: Perhaps a father might tell his child that if the child does not complete their homework by 6pm, then that child might lose their screen privileges for the evening. This would be a way to create a motivational push for the child to do their homework in a timely fashion, and if they cannot meet this deadline, then they lose something they wanted and will learn in the future to work faster.

People who are dieting often set up commitment devices for themselves around food. For example, a dieter might decide that if they abide by their diet plan all week with no cheating, they will be able to go out with friends on Sunday and have drinks they otherwise will not be able to have. If they are tempted throughout the week, they can recall the commitment they have made, and this can help them to persist in their goal.

Strategy #8: The Aggregation of Marginal Gains

Marginal gains are the improvements that occur that might seem insignificant if viewed myopically. However, even if you only improve something by 1%, that 1% will combine with the next 1% improvement, and the next 1% improvement, and the next 1% improvement, and the aggregate, or the combination, will be powerful. This strategy requires a perspective shift that can be helpful in many areas in life. A person doesn't have to do one major life-shattering thing to be successful, in fact, most people's success is a result of these marginal gains in different areas of their life that eventually add up to a large amount.

Don't ever let yourself feel as if the improvements you are making are inconsequential because they are not large enough for others to see and fawn over. If you are consistently working to make improvements in an area, whether it is self-improvement or improvements for your business or home or whatever, it is guaranteed that eventually, the aggregation of these marginal gains will yield big results. Every bit counts.

Strategy #9: Manage Your Energy

The idea behind this strategy is a powerful one: Everyone has the same 24 hours in a day, but not everyone is able to maintain and manage their energy to be as productive as they possibly can in this fixed amount of time. There are many ways to manage your energy, and these include getting an adequate amount of rest at night, be aware of the things that zap your energy and plan accordingly (some people like to space out the tasks they dislike throughout their day, so they do something "easy" than something "hard" than "easy" than "hard" again and so on, but this is individualistic, and everyone has their own preference) and learn your pacing schedule. Are you the type of person who works best in the morning when they've just arrived at the office? Then schedule your most heavy-hitting work for right away so you can take advantage of that energy. If you are someone who feels most motivated after your lunch break, then plan for the heavy-hitting work then. The most important bit here is that you learn what works best for you and take advantage of that information.

Strategy #10: Protect Your Time

This one is important for personal and professional life. Create boundaries for yourself in every area- emails, phone calls, office visits, lunch meetings, etc. You have to be clear and firm with others regarding when you will be available and in what way. This even includes family and friends. You cannot be at the top of your game if your spouse is calling you at 9:30am asking where their favorite thermos is. Protect your time and space, both mentally and physically.

These strategies are all various plans and designs that have worked for one person or another at some point. These strategies are all taught in business schools and entrepreneurship programs and the like, but it does not mean that every single one of them is going to be crucial for your success. Some may resonate more with you than others, and that will be important for you to pay attention to. They all have something to teach, but some will be more important for you to learn from than others.

Chapter 12: How to Build Routines and Habits for Ultimate Self-Discipline Summary Guide

You've made it! Now that you have learned the theories, practices, and strategies for developing the self-discipline skills of willpower, self-control, and mental toughness that are needed to finish what you start and distinguish yourself from others, all that is left now is for you to walk the walk.

Remember that the brain is not a fixed organ. Its neuroplasticity is one of the greatest gifts that humans have, and all we have to do to take advantage of it is to build new neural pathways. Building neural pathways require repetition and consistency with the association, with the positive association being the most powerful. You can build and program the habits of self-discipline into your brain just as a computer programmer would code a new program onto a computer. In order to do this effectively, you must be honest with yourself as you figure out what really pushes your buttons and gets in the way of your self-discipline most of the time. Once you understand your weaknesses, you better know how to strengthen them. The same applies to your discipline drains. Don't let your self-discipline be siphoned off and away.

There are many incredible role-models on this journey towards greater self-discipline, and there is no better model of self-discipline than the US Navy Seal training program. Remember that mental toughness is not something that is born into someone; it is something that is practiced and trained for. It is something anyone can build regardless of their age or status. You can do this by flexing your uncomfortable muscle in a variety of different daily situations. Remember, you are training here! You must take action and use consistency and repetition to build these muscles of willpower, self-control, and mental toughness. Reframing how you think about willpower and building a relationship in which you are using willpower as a tool for success vs. an enemy that must be battled will help you in this.

Creating a disciplined environment will help you to stay on task and focused on your goals, but this is only one piece of the puzzle. What you surround yourself with is important, but what you put in your body is crucial. Remember that you are the director of your life, and your self-control is a muscle that will be strengthened through repetition and reframing. Adopting a growth mindset will work in your favor in any endeavor you pursue, because if you believe that you are incapable of changing yourself and your actions, then you will never succeed. There are numerous strategies on the path to success, and it can be helpful to view the many different strategies you come across as a buffet: take what looks good to you and leave the rest. This does not mean that you should adopt strategies and practices that will challenge you; it only means that not every single strategy may be right for you at this time in your life. Only you will know which strategies and practices will benefit you the most.

Self-discipline is the difference between a person with raw talent that succeeds in life and a person with raw talent that exists somewhere much lower on the barometer of success. Self-discipline is just taking the areas of your life from one level to the next by persistence, consistency, strategy, and know-how. Willpower, self-control, and mental toughness are traits that can be easily developed and strengthened in those who have the interest and drive to do so.

Remember the most beautiful part of self-discipline is that it is entirely up to the person wielding it how it will be used. Will it be a blip on the radar, or will it be a force to be reckoned with? That depends entirely on YOU.

www.ingramcontent.com/pod-product-compliance
Lightning Source LLC
Chambersburg PA
CBHW061710250726
48657CB00002B/580